Education and Contextualism

Education and Contextualism

Architects Design Partnership

black dog
publishing

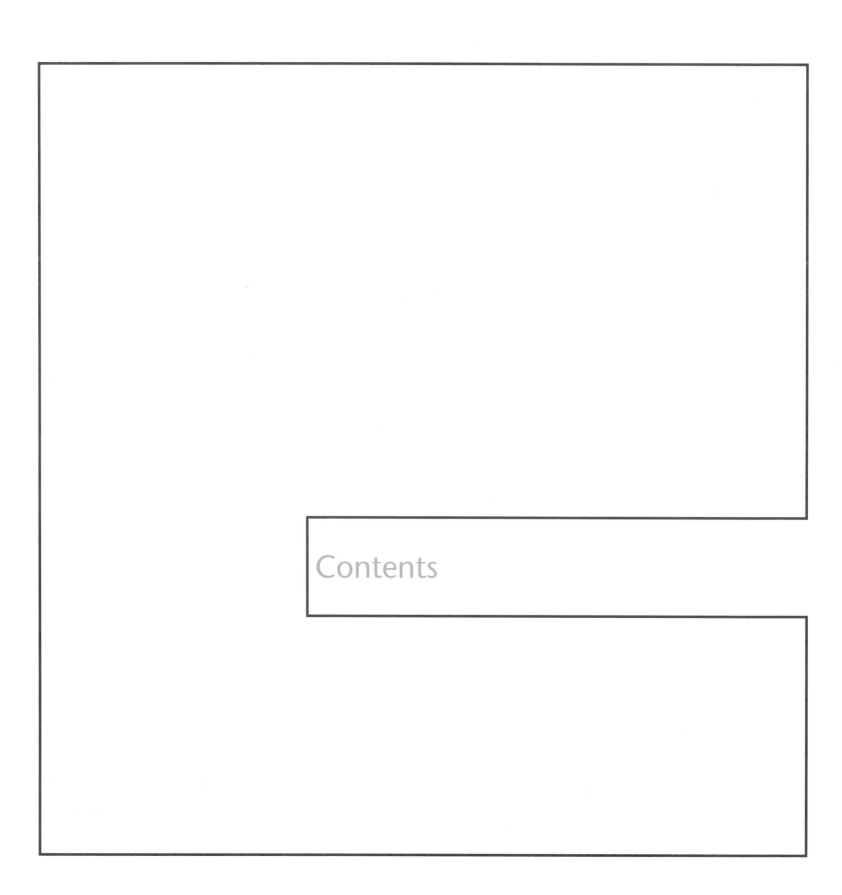

Contents

Introduction

The design of the shape and structure of this book mirrors ADP's approach to architecture. It aims to be useful and practical to the reader, to offer benefit to others. It is also intended to inspire, but not as an end in itself or at the expense of being functional. The practice believes in strong ideas, well executed through careful advanced planning, and this can be applied just as much to the concept for a book as for a building. The book's contents and our philosophy reflect the age in which we live, the context within which we work.

These values go down well with academics and those who represent their interests, enabling the practice to develop a multitude of education-sector clients. Over 40 years ADP has accumulated a wealth of expertise, illustrated in this book, and education projects now represent the main body of our work. This is not a sector that wants short-term fixes or brash attention-seeking statements: it needs well-considered buildings that are based on thorough analysis and understanding of the brief, that are ready when they are needed and do not exceed their budgets, and which attract and inspire those who use them. They may not all make the weekly architectural headlines, but by consistent delivery of these objectives the practice has grown and flourished.

Our buildings share an approach that is diametrically opposed to the headline-making icons of major civic statements or landmark corporate headquarters. With care, everyday buildings can reflect high aspirations, and recurring themes are the appropriateness of solutions and well-mannered contextualism. This approach has found expression in an immense range of projects: specialist facilities such as laboratories, auditoria, swimming pools, music facilities, and also flexible multi-purpose teaching spaces, administration areas and social facilities. We have developed techniques to achieve the best possible value for money, to identify client requirements, and a responsible approach to sustainability. These are discussed and illustrated by reference to a wide range of our work for universities, colleges, and schools.

The fact that this book roughly corresponds with the completion of ADP's 40th year in business is coincidental. The anniversary did make us pause for reflection, but not in the belief that this would be of wider interest beyond our own organisation. Ours is not an organisation with a dominant figurehead or practice style that is imposed on a client or location. To the contrary, just as we analyse and develop every brief as a unique challenge, so each site is individually appraised, leading to bespoke solutions. Again, we find that this brings great user satisfaction but does not necessarily generate a strong stylistic statement. We aim to produce buildings that are responsive to their context and aspire to a timeless quality, rather than following the latest architectural fashions. There is a consistency of approach and philosophy—rather than outcome or expression—which underlie our designs, and these principles are discussed and illustrated. Because these are based on response to context, and the location of our work is diverse, inevitably the end products appear, and are, diverse. However, the process by which we arrive at those solutions is consistent, logical and appropriate. This is examined at a range of scales, from the regional context to the local streetscene, and the importance and impact of detail, choice of materials and colour is discussed. As well as the physical framework, the social context of our buildings is also covered.

In addition to reflecting the differing circumstances of context and programme, our work also represents the contributions of several different partners, operating from various office locations. This too generates a diversity which we regard as an asset, exploiting different individual interests and skills to create a practice greater than the sum of its parts. This takes us back to the philosophy of our founding fathers, who did not call the practice "Hutchings and Fryman" but something capable of renewal as succeeding architects designed in partnership.

The book has been subdivided to cover two main themes: education and contextualism. In general, these are illustrated by reference to built projects: to have been physically realised means that our solutions have successfully navigated the processes of planning, client approval and construction, giving them demonstrable viability. Rarely have we referred to unbuilt schemes. Whilst these are not burdened by the realities of being built—meaning they can be a purer expression of an idea or philosophy—ours is a pragmatic approach, not theory-based.

Architecture is a unique creative act, constrained by others and by time. Architects are a step removed from the actual process of creating built form, indicating through drawings our intentions for execution by others. Furthermore, key ingredients of architecture—form, mass, space and the play of light—cannot be conveyed satisfactorily through drawings… and nor can they be entirely represented by photographs or descriptions in a book. Buildings need to be experienced and used over a period of time to explore how they fulfil their purpose, adapt and change, and contribute to their context.

What we do for a living shapes people's lives and represents a significant responsibility. We take this seriously. We aim to produce buildings which make a positive contribution to their physical context, but also to the lives of those who use them. The most important aspect of this is in relation to the impact of our designs on the environment. Sustainable design is no longer an optional extra.

This book begins by looking at the history and origins of the practice. It then examines the present by describing our current portfolio of education-sector projects and contextual approach. Finally, we look to the future, and the approach we are taking to sustainable design.

This would be incomplete without a few words of thanks: to our many clients who have provided us with the opportunities represented on these pages (and countless schemes we have been unable to include); to all the staff of ADP who have worked so hard to produce them; and to the other consultants and contractors with whom we have worked to realise them in practice.

Roger FitzGerald

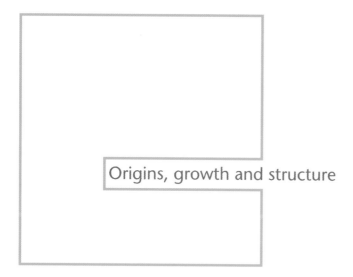

Origins, growth and structure

On 12 June 1962 John Fryman wrote to a neighbouring practice, run by Victor Hutchings, suggesting that they should amalgamate their two businesses: "It seems to me in this day of mergers, takeovers, supermarkets, consortiums and SfB's that it could do no harm for us to be more than practising neighbours!"

At the time, John was operating out of Marlow, and Victor from Henley on Thames and London. There was a symmetry between the two organisations: both had been running their own practices for a few years, and both had four assistants. Both had worked for well-known established architectural offices before they set-up on their own: John for Yorke, Rosenberg and Mardall (YRM) and Victor for Lord Esher (Lionel Brett).

Architecture, and life generally, were buoyant and optimistic, with the success of the Festival of Britain and confidence in the future. Following lengthy discussions through 1964 and 1965 it was finally agreed to join forces.

What was happening in 1965 when the practice was founded? In this year, Sir Winston Churchill died, The Beatles received MBEs, the Post Office Tower opened as the tallest building in the UK, hemlines continued to rise, and Cliff Richard was in the Top Ten. Le Corbusier died, in August.

This was a time when names like Building Design Partnership and Architects Co-Partnership were becoming popular, and individuals' names were being dropped. The new practice wanted to call itself Associated Architects—AA—to be at the top of any directory, but the Business Names Registration would not agree to this and so, after eliminating many other possibilities, the name Architects Design Partnership (ADP) was finally chosen.

During this time, Victor Hutchings was acting for a client whose projects included the conversion of Denmark House, a listed town house close to the centre of Henley, into flats. It was agreed that this would make an ideal office instead, and the founding partners bought the premises from their client. In July 1965 alteration works began

In the 1960s, when Architects Design Partnership was formed, confidence was high, construction work gathered pace with bold modern architecture, and culture was dominated by The Beatles (seen above with their MBEs).

and were complete in time to allow the business to start trading from Denmark House on 1 October 1965. The offices were decorated in the fashionable colours of the time—various shades of grey—and subsequent refurbishments encompassed colour changes reflecting the preferences of the time, with the 1970s marked by a brown, beige and orange scheme.

Commissions were generally quite small but a growing reputation led to work with Oxford University Press and Oxford colleges. Strong relationships developed, based on close mutual trust and confidence, and became an integral part of ADP's philosophy.

Amongst John Fryman's assistants was John Kempster, and amongst Victor's there was David Mitchell. These two, together with Michael Thomas (who joined the practice in 1967), became the second generation of partners, in 1975. ADP was expanding, developing its reputation in the Thames Valley, with satellite offices in London and Oxford.

Denmark House, the refurbished building in Henley on Thames, where the practice was first established.

From the outset, ADP worked for education-sector clients such as Jesus College, Oxford. Designs were modernist, but took account of their neighbours and settings, such as the new Old Members' Building for Jesus College (left). The College marked its 400th anniversary with this new building in 1970–1971, providing study bedrooms, seminar rooms, workshops and a roof top music room. A shop (WH Smith and Sons) fronting Cornmarket is an integral part of the scheme.

High quality materials—Clipsham limestone, lead, bronze and glass—provide enduring characteristics whilst the projecting glass bays make a contemporary addition to the College. The scheme was extended to the rear in 1989 with the addition of a larger conference room, the Habakkuk Room.

A priority of the original briefing information was that the project should contribute positively to its historic setting, and the building fulfils this requirement.

ADP's reputation for high quality contextual design grew in the late 1960s and early 1970s with wide coverage of its work in central Oxford for the colleges, such as the Old Members' Building for Jesus College (below and right), and the Weir Common Room for University College (opposite page).

Repetitive precast concrete panels enabled the Institute of Hydrology, in Wallingford, to be rapidly constructed. The plan arrangement allowed for alternative internal wall configurations, derived from various office sizes to suit different grades of staff (entitlement according to grade). As well as cellular office areas, larger open plan laboratories, office and computer suites were created in two-storey blocks, with public areas such as library, seminar and dining rooms situated in single-storey wings. The two are arranged around courtyards.

The work of the practice was diverse, undertaking commissions for local individuals and businesses in the Henley area, local authorities, several Research Councils, an impressive list of Oxford colleges, Oxford University Press, Henley Management College, and work in the healthcare sector. This diversity helped ADP withstand fluctuations such as the sudden termination of all hospital work in the 1970s.

Circumstances in the industry helped shape architectural concepts so, for example, when there was a brick shortage in the early 1970s we responded by designing the Institute of Hydrology in precast concrete. More iconic designs, influenced by the High-Tech movement, followed, most notably for the Water Research Council in Swindon. The Wave Basin Building in Wallingford was similarly confident, with a strong expression of structure and cladding bringing life and interest to a straightforward brief.

The new complex for Hydraulics Research in Wallingford, on the banks of the Thames, provides a large wave basin research facility, exhibition and display areas, a lecture theatre, offices and a computer suite. The main structure is steel, chosen because it is capable of the long spans required, was within the budget, and met the demands of a fast-track programme.

A main lightweight truss spans the full length of the building and this is echoed by the main entrance and central circulation. Portal frames span onto the truss on either side, enclosing the accommodation. By avoiding supporting columns, the structural solution provides the client with total flexibility.

The building was divided into two elements—the research area and the rest of the accommodation—and the truss, by spanning everything, unifies the two.

The engineering complex in Swindon, for the Water Research Centre, is clad with demountable and interchangeable glass fibre panels in strident blue and red colours, which can be unbolted and exchanged.

The building houses laboratories, an experimental hall, and offices on either side of a glazed spine which contains communal facilities.

Origins, growth and structure

To maximise flexibility of the layouts, at the Water Research Centre in Swindon, the main structural columns were taken outside the building envelope and expressed as giant tubular elements. The central atrium provided a social heart to the building, where scientists could meet informally, before returning to their cellular offices and laboratories.

During the 1970s and 1980s ADP was still best known for its work in Oxfordshire and the Thames Valley. By 1980 the practice had grown to approximately 30 staff and numbers increased further when a small office was established in Yeovil in 1986, initially to service a large Property Services Agency (PSA) contract at *HMS Osprey*, in Portland. In addition to its core work, ADP ventured into the Middle East, undertaking projects for the Suez Canal Authority—the Port Said Shipyard Training Centre—and a traffic police headquarters in Abu Dhabi.

Having been founded in the heady days of the mid-1960s, tougher times lay ahead. The industry became notably more commercial, epitomised by the Royal Institute of British Architects' legal advisor of the time, who stated "clients are no longer gentlemen, contractors are no longer gentlemen, and it's about time architects stopped thinking they are gentlemen". Other changes included Lord Denning's statement on unlimited liability, the dropping of the mandatory fee scales, and granting the right to advertise. One change (which was particularly noted when the practice celebrated its 25th anniversary in 1990) was metrication: not an obviously significant event, but likened to having to learn and use a new language halfway through your career.

In 1990, two new third-generation partners were appointed: David Heslop in Oxford and Roger FitzGerald in London. Almost simultaneously, the industry entered a major recession but as building work recovered so the practice emerged stronger and with increasing work outside its original territory. The London and Oxford bases grew whilst the work local to Henley on Thames diminished. Eventually the inevitable decision was made to close the office where ADP began.

In the 1990s the practice avoided the then populist but rapidly dated postmodernist style, preferring to remain true to its principles of finding appropriate solutions to the client's needs and deriving expression from the building's function and the context in which it was located. Awards followed for both new build and refurbishment schemes, including a new quadrangle for Christ Church Oxford, refurbishment of Reading Town Hall, and a private swimming pool by the River Thames.

Less celebrated, but arguably more valued and worthy, was a series of hospice projects throughout the country. These are quietly understated, providing a homely and welcoming environment for patients and relatives at a time when they need support. A strong concept was produced for this with many buildings organised around a central space, inspired by the way that the village green acts as the circulation hub and social centre for a village.

This project for Christ Church in Oxford won an RIBA National Award and the jury described the contextual approach: "The prime aim of the architect selected in competition for this project was to achieve a low key, harmonious infill along two major facades. This has been achieved in a very sensitive manner at the same time securing a practical solution with spacious rooms well liked by the users and those who produced the briefs… The setting, landscaping and external pavings are also excellent".

Overleaf
Working with Cancer Relief (Macmillan Fund), ADP developed a design concept for a national programme for the provision of Day Care and Hospice units. Ward areas, day care facilities, education and support functions were arranged around a central communal area. This concept allowed for standardisation in terms of meeting technical requirements, but enough flexibility to allow for a response to the surrounding site and needs of the local health authority. Knowledge gained could be applied to a number of independent hospices, such as St Margaret's in Yeovil.

As the practice emerged from the recession, it identified the education sector as an area where government spending would be needed, and this has become one of the practice's main specialisms. Two more partners were appointed as the first and second generation partners retired; first James Middleton-Stewart, in 1997 and then Alison McKerracher, in 2003. Also, a new office was opened in Birmingham in 2000.

In 2002 the practice undertook major structural change, converting from a partnership structure—individuals working together—to a Limited Liability Partnership (LLP), a legal entity in itself. This also created the opportunity to develop a different, more corporate structure, in which ownership and strategic management could be separated from client management.

FitzGerald, Heslop, Middleton-Stewart and McKerracher remained as owners, fulfilling roles in all but name as Chairman, Managing Director, Company Secretary and Director of Human Resources, whilst new appointments were made of partners to deal with client and local office management: Chris Thornton in Yeovil, Simon Kneafsey in Oxford, soon followed by Bruce Mullett (Oxford), Jon Roylance (Birmingham, now Manchester) and Nichola Wood (London), and then in 2007 Nick Woodcock and Jason Curran (both Birmingham). This fourth generation of partners within an LLP structure gave the practice yet more credibility and capacity to widen its clientele, whilst maintaining a core value: that of close partner involvement throughout the life of a project.

As a result ADP has continued its growth trend, with its staff list expanding to approaching 100, and by rising a few more places (to 34) in the 2006 *Architects' Journal* Top 100 Practices. New sectors of work are being explored and cultivated to supplement our expertise in education, and complementary skills developed, such as the creation of a new interiors division. The most recent development is the opening of an office in Manchester in 2007.

The two main themes of this book, our education sector work and our concern for designing to suit the context in which new architecture is found, reflect the practice's current work and design philosophy. They have emerged naturally from the first origins of the practice and the principles on which it was founded. Even in the early 1980s ADP was promoting the use of recycled paper, sustainable materials for thermal insulation, and the responsible specification of building products. The issue of sustainability has become ever more influential, and we discuss this further in the final, forward-looking chapter.

top left
Oriental Pearl Restaurant in Birmingham

top right and bottom
Brunel University

ADP uses strong colour, effective use of lighting, careful choice of materials and a well researched furniture selection to create vibrant and imaginative interiors that provide timeless quality married with practical and functional space. Since it was formed in 2004, the ADP Interiors Division has undertaken a range of significant and high profile projects, including conference centres, business schools, restaurants, and hotels.

Through an imaginative and carefully researched choice of materials, meticulous attention to detail, and confident use of colour and lighting, ADP creates practical and contemporary spaces that are dynamic and attractive for regular users and visitors. At the Aston Business School Conference Centre three accent colours were used: black, cranberry and lime green. These run through the entire project, from the boutique-style bedrooms to the restaurant, bar and even the uniforms worn by staff.

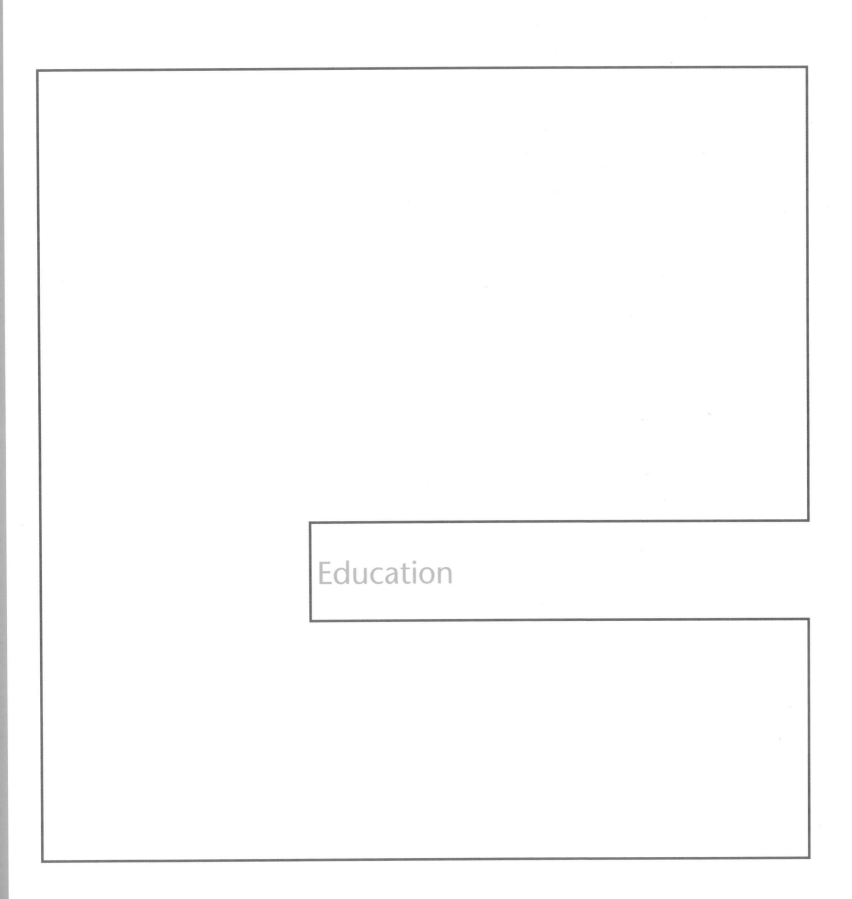

Education

Slough Borough Council encouraged an imaginative design for Western House Primary School, aiming towards an award-winning standard, while also remaining conscious of the running costs and the practical needs of the school community. The building is a landmark within the community and accentuates this key corner site, while also being sustainable by using natural ventilation and the responsible selection of materials. It has promoted a sense of pride in the local community, and provides a focal point for the surrounding residential area.

By the 1990s, Architects Design Partnership had developed a diverse portfolio of work across a variety of sectors: education, research, public sector, leisure, residential, healthcare and commercial. Whilst the practice has continued to be active in all these areas, increasingly clients are looking to appoint consultants with specialist knowledge in their field.

We recognised this and have developed a strong expertise in education sector work. Within this, there is still great diversity, and sub-groups within the sector operate in their own particular way: a university is quite different from a further education college; an independent school from one run by a local authority.

At the same time, there are common themes: the need for flexibility, the incorporation of e-learning, the need for strategic long-term planning and the need for efficient use of space.

This chapter therefore focuses on this major sector of ADP's current work, exploring some of the differences, of process and building type, between client groupings whilst also finding some of the common themes that transcend the whole sector.

The buildings of an educational institution play a large part in encouraging pride in students, staff, and the wider community, and the quality of the environment can have a profound effect on the educational standards provided. A central challenge to designers is to produce buildings and spaces that inspire users while working within tight budgets and timeframes.

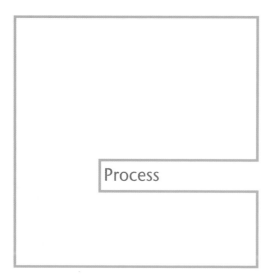

Process

Capital projects are invariably about change. Why would any institution want to spend considerable amounts of capital merely to recreate the status quo? However, undertaking change in educational establishments can be even more difficult than in other types of organisation, as a clear definition of what is driving change can become obscured by the sector's traditional debating culture.

The diverse nature of education-sector work makes the interface between professional teams (architects, engineers, cost consultants, and so on) and clients variable across sub-sectors (for example schools, colleges, and universities), and even within them, as complexities in the nature and type of institution arise. Governance and management structures differ between and within sub-sectors, thus providing for a rich mixture of decision-making cultures and processes: this can vary almost to the level of the individual institution.

Appropriate techniques need to be developed, and constantly re-evaluated, to deal with this range of very specific processes. ADP spends much time in thinking about and planning how to integrate its architectural service with the requirements of education clients. The education sector provides a unique and stimulating challenge to the designer, and success is only achieved with an understanding of the infrastructure and operational imperatives that apply.

In higher education there will usually be a senior member of the institution who takes executive or board level responsibility as a champion for estates development and masterplanning, typically a pro vice-chancellor. This person may well not be an expert in the field of design or construction but they will be expected to understand the overall aims of the university, and to lead the translation of these into future plans for the development of the estate and physical learning environment. In this work the pro vice-chancellor will usually be supported by an experienced estates department and finance regime, plus external professionals and a cross section of senior stakeholders, in order to create initially costed and logistically feasible plans. The proposals will then be presented to a senior group, such as a university executive, for support before going on to a board of governors or a senate for final approval.

A detailed knowledge of the requirements of higher education projects, developed over four decades, has allowed the practice to build strong relationships with various universities, such as the University of Birmingham where it has carried out a series of projects over the past decade. Examples are provided throughout this book; the building to the left is the Net Shape Building.

When decisions are made regarding professional teams for individual or groups of capital projects, the process is usually devolved to and led by the pro vice-chancellor or director of estates, with appropriate input from current stakeholders in the facility to be created. The recommendations of this group are then presented to the Board for final ratification.

This decision-making and management culture extends into the delivery of capital projects. Individual institutions will operate with different mixes of professional teams, often based on internal preference and also on procurement route. The professional teams interface with the institution through the estates department.

Overall the decision-making process in higher education is independent of external influences. However, the governing body or senate has responsibility for ensuring that the institution is managed appropriately, and both external and internal auditors are required to monitor decisions and processes with regard to good practice on behalf of

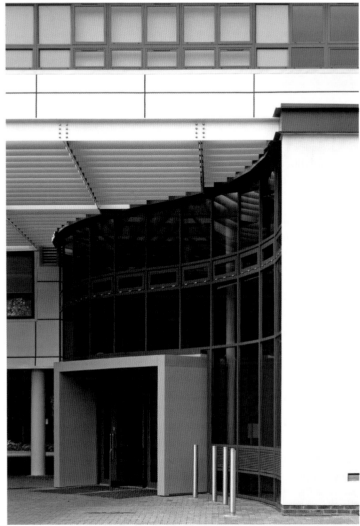

Located in the heart of the Ealing Studios and Media Village, this is Ealing, Hammersmith and West London College's Centre of Vocational Excellence in Media and Visual Arts. An outer 'shell' of heavily textured brickwork responds to the local park and neighbouring Grade I listed Pitshanger Manor, by Sir John Soane. Within these surroundings the building reveals smooth and metallic surfaces (illustrated), including a suspended metallic mesh which faces towards Ealing Green and onto which images can be projected (left).

The project was developed in close consultation with the Learning and Skills Council (LSC), and included frequent meetings with the Finance and Estates Departments, and regular formal reports to the College's Estates and Capital Project Committee.

the Higher Education Funding Council (HEFCE). This gives universities the autonomy necessary to define their own direction while ensuring appropriate management of decision-making, financial planning and the operation of the institution.

In further education the situation is somewhat different. The local representation of the Learning and Skills Council (LSC) is responsible for funding major capital projects within a regional plan. This puts an extra layer into the decision-making process, but on the other hand is designed to co-ordinate the provision and development of further education within an individual Learning and Skills Council area.

Further education colleges will generally have their own estates department. However, this often concentrates mainly on the estates maintenance and finance role and does not always have the capacity to take on masterplanning. In this case the college will usually engage a project manager for the duration of the project, to support and advise college management and the internal team and to take a client-side lead on many of the technical issues.

Given the role of the Learning and Skills Council, decision-making naturally becomes a two-stage process. The first stage involves the college in making an initial proposal to the LSC in order to gain in-principle support for the project. This proposal will summarise the strategic need for the project and provide outline plans and projected costs; this needs a significant amount of academic and technical input and requires the college to engage a professional design team.

Once LSC support is forthcoming, the next stage depends on the size of the project. If it is a large-scale project or campus masterplan, the work will generally need to be re-tendered through the Official Journal of the European Union (OJEU) process. For smaller projects this may not be necessary, in which case the initial professional team may well be asked to continue.

The project is finally taken to full design and costing and resubmitted to the LSC for approval. It is at this stage that funding is secured and the project can proceed to procurement. Throughout the process a senior member of the college, usually the principal or a deputy, will take responsibility for the project. As is the case in the higher education sector, the senior manager responsible will not necessarily be an expert in capital projects and they probably do not have the level of specialist technical support available to their university counterparts.

Although the college senior team will take internal responsibility for the development of the work, it is likely that the college board of governors will also take an active role in order to discharge their governance responsibilities and to support the senior and professional teams. In addition the college's auditors and the LSC will also continue to play a monitoring role with regard to process and to ensuring value for money.

The decision-making process in further education with regard to capital projects is somewhat more externally monitored and controlled than that in higher education. The college board of governors tends to take a more proactive role and the LSC, as the funding body, is involved not only in monitoring good practice and value for money but also in making the major funding decisions.

The schools sector functions differently. Although the further and higher education sectors can be viewed as having many differing institution types within them, they do only have single funding bodies and therefore single sets of imperatives and guidance with regard to the implementation of capital programmes. In the schools sector, governance and funding can vary in a number of ways; this situation is propounded by government initiatives which add further complexities. At present and into the medium term these initiatives mean that it is appropriate to consider three of the sub-categories of school, those being the state schools involved in the Schools of the Future project (where the professional could either give direct advice as a specialist design advisor to a client, or as part of a contractor team bidding to provide a package of several phased new schools), the School Academies, and the Independent sector in its various forms.

The government's Building Schools for the Future (BSF) programme is concerned with the refurbishment or rebuilding of schools across the state sector in order to create fit-for-purpose provision, and is being implemented in four basic phases. The schools (usually led by the headteacher) within a local authority are grouped into a 'wave' and the local authority then takes responsibility for defining and organising the programme to be undertaken.

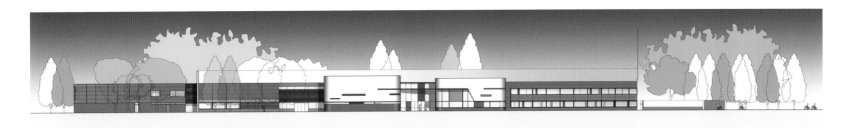

Given that schools will not generally have the technical knowledge or the spare resource to undertake such a programme, the local authority becomes involved in the design and procurement process. Professional teams for given projects are chosen from an approved list, for which a tender process is engaged. A number of central initiatives have also been undertaken in an attempt to create 'standard' off-the-shelf designs for features such as sports halls and even for schools themselves; these designs can then be personalised for the particular school or location in order to minimise design time and overall costs.

With these projects the school governors and senior team clearly need to have a critical input regarding the functionality and fitness-for-purpose of the design. However, the major decisions regarding the professional team and procurement lie with the local authority.

In the case of academies a commercial sponsor has to be in place. This individual or organisation is required to guarantee a substantial financial contribution to the project before government approval is gained. As for the BSF programme it is unlikely that

ADP has recently been successful in winning the Leicester BSF programme, with Miller Construction, where the practice's primary role is to develop and co-ordinate the designs for two schools as well as developing the client's requirements with an educational specialist.

Our experience in working with clients, local authorities, user groups and key stakeholders has been critical here, reconciling a multiplicity of aspirations with the practicalities of delivering projects on-time and on-budget, in order to fulfil contractor requirements and ensure the success of the schemes.

the senior team in the academy will have the time or expertise to manage the project: however in this case the academy will appoint the professional team with advice from the local authority and from the sponsor. The sponsors will also require a major say in the project; depending on the nature of the sponsorship, this involvement can vary from extreme 'hands-on' to largely 'hands-off'.

The independent school sector is largely outside the local authority decision-making process. In this case funding is from a variable mixture of using part of overall fee income, and fundraising campaigns targeting former pupils, current parents, and wealthy benefactors. Therefore, although the school will be subject to external audit or inspection on aspects of governance, management and financial processes, its decision-making will be far more autonomous that other parts of the schools sector. In the case of decisions around capital projects the school will rely on the bursar and headteacher for day-to-day management, with some technical input from the buildings and grounds maintenance team. The professional team will then generally be appointed by the governors, with advice from the school senior team.

ADP has maintained a close working relationship with Highgate School in London, and has undertaken a range of projects including the refurbishment and extension of School House (illustrated), and the roof extension of the Science Block. This has enabled the practice to help shape Highgate's future plans, integrating building projects with the needs and aspirations of a changing educational establishment.

Significantly extended at lower ground floor level, the building seems largely unaltered when viewed across playing fields (left).

Internal alterations provide contemporary additions to the traditional interior (opposite).

Priorities

When undertaking capital projects in the education sector it is vital to fully understand and work with the priorities of the institution and the requirements of the particular project. These key aims can be many and varied depending on the nature of the work.

Within an institution itself there will be a number of priorities, some or all of which will apply to a particular project. One classification could be the environment, within which examples of possible priorities could be: the learning environment, resources and facilities for the student body; the working environment for staff; the research provision and facilities; the social and social learning context; and the opportunities for community involvement.

In addition, the institution or project will have a set of generic 'business' priorities. These are likely to include some or all of: value for money, coupled to effectiveness and/or efficiency; the reinforcement of a 'brand' or image; the creation of a 'statement' or 'iconic' facility; the creation of marketing advantage; sustainability; resilience of systems and facilities; safety, security and access.

ADP's work over the past ten years with Cokethorpe School has assisted it in identifying key priorities and opportunities in response to an ever-changing and competitive marketplace in which an independent school operates. We have assisted the School with strategic planning through masterplan and conservation plan studies, and the implementation of specific building projects such as the new Learning Resource Centre (illustrated), new teaching block and library together with significant areas of landscaping.

The masterplan and individual building projects have allowed the School to develop a clear strategy for growth on a sensitive conservation site. Future development has been broken down into clear projects that can be integrated into the working school environment with minimum disruption to students and staff.

Although these priorities may seem self-evident, it is critical that objectives, and their relative importance, are established at project definition and initiation in order to avoid confusion and potential conflict later in the process. It is at this point that the 'debating culture' of education establishments can either be an asset or a risk to a project. If the client group is being appropriately managed within the institution there is the likelihood that a clear set of priorities will have been established, and positive ownership of the project achieved.

However, if this has not happened there is a real possibility that the client group will not arrive at an agreed position; this then tends to lead to a lack of ownership and even disowning of the project.

Regardless of the initial project specification, it is therefore important that the design team conduct an early review with the decision-makers in the client team in order to confirm and develop the brief to such a point that a 'sign off' occurs. The agreed brief, including identification of priorities which the project must achieve, then provides both the client and the design team with a clear point of reference as the project develops. This may seem like an obvious position to seek; however, given the dynamic intellectual culture of academia, without such an agreement individuals are likely to seek to influence or change the specification, which can lead to conflict and to potential cost to the client.

In any environment it is advisable to have clear and unambiguous lines of communication and defined levels of authority between the client and the design team as the project progresses. This is particularly important in the education sector, where the accepted freedom of action within the normal culture can easily lead to attempted interference in the project by well-intentioned groups or individuals. This leads to significant challenges for the design team as they work to preserve clarity of the priorities within the project.

The team should understand and evaluate the client brief and from this produce a design that meets the client's requirements in terms of functionality, priorities, branding, affordability and value for money. They should then ensure that the facility is actually created to deliver the client's requirements and the design philosophy.

However, from the client's viewpoint the contribution is also expected to be of a more personal and developmental nature, requiring not only technical skills but also leadership, management and often visionary inputs in order to deliver the full potential of a project. This is particularly true in the education sector, where there is real opportunity to harness the experience and aspirations of different groups in order to achieve unexpected but valuable benefits that actually take the institution, or even the sector, forwards. This can be understood as introducing the 'stretch' into a project, which challenges thinking both within the client team and the design team in ways that make real innovation possible.

The University of Birmingham West Campus Project, completed in July 2002, exemplifies ADP's ability to provide innovative solutions to a project. This project also demonstrates our commitment to delivering sustainable building solutions and minimising environmental impact.

ADP worked in tandem with senior personnel at the University to develop strategic objectives, then translated these, (first in a design competition) then through the detailed implementation, into a new masterplan for a complete section of the University, incorporating a new arrival sequence for the pedestrian approaching the University from the railway station. A proactive and creative approach integrated the detailed development of the brief and early design concepts—for example, ensuring that the building could easily adapt in the future to different uses. Forward-thinking strategies for the positioning and sizing of staircases and toilet cores, the structural, servicing and fire strategies, all ensure that the scheme will be easily adapted in the future: inherently sustainable, by maximising the future use and life of the building.

The West Campus project at the University of Birmingham. At the outset we worked with the University to identify priorities and objectives, then ensured that the project achieved these requirements.

Clients are always keen to employ designers with specific relevant experience. Over time this could lead to the formation of exclusive groups of designers, not only across the sector but within particular, difficult-to-access sub-markets, potentially leading to staleness in the design and development of educational facilities. It is a given that clients expect design competence from the team. In many cases it is not just the technical competence required to produce the design; it is also the design team's role in the process of design delivery that is important. The knowledge and comfort that the design team has experience of, and understands how to work within, the sector or sub-sector is usually a major consideration when appointing the team.

The education sector does not stand still in its thinking and this clearly applies to the estates and facilities where educational practice takes place. Educational technologies are developing at an increasing pace and along with this goes a rapidly developing understanding of pedagogy and the requirements of learners. This directly impacts on the design of educational environments, requiring high priority to be given to creativity not only in the spaces for today but also in the creation of environments that are going to be adaptable and flexible enough to stand the test of ever changing times.

Students and staff are also demanding quality in the design of the environments where they study, work and socialise. The days when rows of desks in bland spaces were the acceptable norm have long gone. It is increasingly important to instil quality and create a feeling of pride and ownership in the institution.

These issues are a direct challenge to a design team and create major expectations around creativity and design quality in the client to design team relationship. In the education sector there is a strong argument that, with regard to design, it is what young people do rather than what older people say or think that matters. This leads to the somewhat revolutionary sentiment that 'designers and clients should have 18 year old mentors'.

The education sector as a whole has clearly developed a set of values and requirements that it wishes to see in its design teams. These transcend the obvious and expected requirement for technical competence and move into areas such as understanding the sector and the creation of long term relationships and personal service in order to harvest the benefits of this mutual understanding.

In the environment of educational establishments, softer skills such as negotiation, problem solving, project management and change management are also important to the client as they seek the comfort of appointing a team that will effectively manage and deliver the project to the required vision and specification. Critical in this delivery is the design team's creativity and quality of design, which is necessary to take opportunities to move the institution forward, enhance its profile and reputation and future-proof its facilities in times of rapid change and development.

Masterplanning and strategic thinking

A campus masterplan will involve a wide range of building types: the creation of student and staff residences, specialist facilities for a number of academic disciplines, social and recreational areas, and a variety of learning spaces, business facilities and staff work areas. Such a masterplan will also need to take account of the environment, vehicular and pedestrian movement, transportation, and servicing, the spaces between the buildings, campus logistics, the priorities of the institution, and branding and image. This will need to be implemented in conjunction with an IT infrastructure, sustainability and factors such as building management and the development of an 'intelligent' institution.

Such a masterplan will clearly take many years to deliver, will need a personal empathy between the client and the design team and will need continuity of thought from the team in order to gain the benefits of overall strategic thinking. Not all projects are as large or long as this, but it is still the case that a relationship beyond the individual project is beneficial to the client, because there will continue to be enhancements, refurbishments and adaptations that become necessary. A long-term relationship, with a personal service, is the most appropriate way for the client to achieve such developments.

The process outlined in this chapter describes how strategic thinking extends into masterplanning an institution. This is particularly relevant to university and college campuses, but is also relevant to individual schools. Schools are no longer regarded as closed institutions but are rightly seen as valued assets for all local people. The quality of the environment is also widely considered to play a significant part in shaping the outlook and behaviour of the young people who inhabit it: the external spaces and their relationship with the internal functions of the buildings make an important contribution in this respect. New schools and colleges need the best in building and landscape architecture brought together as integrated design solutions.

Campuses should therefore be distinctive, acting as beacons of design excellence, making a real contribution to the quality of the local built environment. Successful masterplanning of a school may involve the engagement of students, local people and other stakeholders in the planning and design process, and therefore in this situation the designer requires particular expertise in the management and facilitation of community participation programmes.

The creation of a masterplan incorporates knowledge in landscape design and implementation from other areas of the built environment which share many common issues; particularly in respect to spatial hierarchies, security, pedestrian, traffic conflicts and the creation of a distinctive sense of place.

ADP is working with the University of Sussex on a long term (25 year) strategy for its Falmer campus to help it to achieve its growth and academic targets. The site was developed in the early 1960s to the vision of Sir Basil Spence and his work has been recognised by being listed for its iconic architecture. ADP's masterplan develops the best aspects of Spence's early work, exploiting the stunning Downland landscape, and creating usable and attractive courtyards.

More sustainable transport will be encouraged and the road and car parking layouts enhanced. The poorest building stock will be improved or replaced, and lighting, disabled access, signage and bicycle parking carefully integrated. A consistent palette of material will be used and design guidelines provided for all new buildings.

The practice has engaged in an extensive consultation process, within the University, with the local authorities and English Heritage. The Commission for Architecture and the Built Environment describe the proposals as "extremely encouraging", and the first phase of 232 study bedrooms is now under construction to ADP's design.

Strategic thinking

In education, as in any sector, 'strategy' is at the core of thinking when considering the development of an organisation. But how is strategy developed and how are strategic objectives defined and delivered? More importantly, where does the estate fit in?

To start at the top, the institution needs to have a vision or mission to define its values and its overall brand. What is being defined, at the highest level, is what the institution aspires to be. These vision or mission statements, which are often unnecessarily long and obtuse, rarely prove to be the vehicle for real differentiation; this comes later in the strategic thinking process. What they should do is position the institution within its sector, so that major future decisions around strategic objectives can be considered in relation to this position.

What is common about these statements is that they are not usually measurable. So how does the institution, or anyone else, know if the vision is really being achieved what progress is actually being made and to what effect?

This is where the strategic thinking really starts. It is also where an integrated and comprehensive view of the institution develops, which then enables leadership and management to be effective. The organisation needs to come together to create a set of strategic objectives, that relate back to the vision and against which progress is able to be measured. This set of strategic objectives needs to encompass the whole organisation and will need to be delivered in a co-ordinated and structured way.

As part of the Building Schools for the Future process, ADP has worked extensively with Fullhurst Community College to identify stategic ways in which their existing school environment could be transformed, both educationally and in terms of bricks and mortar. This part new-build, part refurbishment scheme takes on board the College's need to retain the old assembly hall building, transforming this into a new atrium space which forms the new social 'heart' of the building. These open, accessible spaces also ensure that children do not feel isolated by their environment, reducing the risk of bullying or fear of social exclusion. Two new resource centres flank a new main entrance area located at the rear of the existing site—improving access and circulation for students and staff. The architecture and organisation of space have evolved from a strategic review of how a secondary school should operate.

An integrated and co-ordinated set of strategic plans come together to deliver the strategic objectives and hence the vision. These plans develop sub-strategies and are used to facilitate tactical decision-making and to define the operational projects that will be required. In a major institution this set of strategic plans can be quite large; from these will emerge the estates masterplan and estates strategies. Strategic plans would typically include those for:

- academic developments
- finance
- learning and teaching
- research
- estates masterplanning
- estates
- information technology
- human resource development
- external income generation
- regional and national role
- international development
- business infrastructure.

Important to this whole strategic thinking process is that it is regularly reviewed in order to make sure that the vision or mission is still relevant, that the objectives still support the mission and that the tactical thinking and operational projects will deliver the objectives.

It is critical in strategic thinking that the human or cultural factors are not ignored. As projects are specified, designed and implemented, it is important that the clients are engaged, because there is often inherent resistance to change—even when that change is understood and supported. Essentially, building projects are about change and change management, with workshops, consultations, brainstorms, process reviews, training and staff development all playing a significant role in ensuring successful engagement by the client group.

Masterplanning

Masterplanning is very much part of the strategic planning of an institution and derives from the overall strategic plan and objectives. In the case of the physical estate, the masterplan will be one of a number of high-level strategic plans and will need to be co-ordinated and integrated with these to create the overall institutional action plan.

The estates masterplan defines the 'route' for the institution's estate over time. Overall it must be academically led in nature and co-ordinated with the other high level strategic plans of the institution; however the technical design nature of much of the work means it would be unusual for the institution not to require external professional support.

This external professional support normally falls into two basic areas: a design team (usually architect-led), and cost consultancy. Project management is also often provided externally and, depending on the overall mix of the team, an experienced domain expert to support decision-making is also valuable if this resource is not available internally.

The estates masterplanning team will usually be led by a senior member of the institution, with strategic responsibility for estates development within the overall strategic framework. The internal team will then include membership ideally from: estates, IT services, learning and teaching specialists, finance and the academic, student and administrative communities. The full team can become rather large, which could lead to a dilution in direction and lack of progress. Therefore, decisive leadership is essential and sub-structures or task and finish groups are often created to facilitate progress.

The academic strategy will analyse student numbers and plan future targets across the institution. From this information projected subject, academic and support staff numbers can be determined. The estates strategy can take these numbers and, by applying recommended space norms, estimate the total estate required to provide general teaching and learning facilities and subject-based staff facilities across the institution. Other strategies such as learning and teaching, research, external income generation and business infrastructure then contribute to determine the total estate required by the institution.

In the case of further education colleges, those attending part time need to be transferred into 'full-time equivalent' students. For independent schools, the number of boarders will be as critical as the quantum of day pupils. In both independent and state school sectors, the profile of the sixth form in relation to the lower school will be significant.

This calculation of required total estate is the initial point to arrive at in appraising the options for the estates masterplan. It is a theoretical figure that will generally be too small, unless optimal fit into existing and ultimately planned buildings can be achieved. For example, the optimum efficient arrangement of teaching space in a secondary school would consist of specialist spaces—such as science laboratories,

NORTH

KEY

☐ CYCLE PATH
▨ MAIN CIRCULATION ROUTES
▨ NEW BUILD - ACADEMIC
☐ NEW BUILD - OTHER
▨ CIRCULAR TROLLEY/ SERVICE ROUTE
▨ 'NODE'
▨ WOODLAND PLANTING
▨ PARKLAND PLANTING
☐ GRASSLAND/SPORTS PITCHES
▨ CURRENT PROPOSALS

design technology workshops, art and music rooms—and standard classrooms for all general subjects that do not need special spaces. By 'booking' the classrooms and careful timetabling, the standard classrooms can be used very efficiently. There is much resistance to this, with a strong preference for teachers to have a classroom base and for subject areas to have a distinct departmental definition. The price for this is a degree of excess space, and acceptance that rooms will not be fully utilised.

Applying the figures to the actual estate and its current usage enables the creation of initial options around fitness for purpose, actual fit into premises, campus mix and integrity in order to provide appropriate academic, learning, business, working and social opportunities.

ADP won a competitive interview for the preparation of a new masterplan for the Hatfield Campus of the University of Hertfordshire. Working with the University, the team addressed a range of issues, including the relationship with a nearby new PFI-funded campus, bus routes, parking, cycle paths, disabled access, expansion and new arrival spaces, landscaping, infrastructure and future flexibility. The masterplan has now been integrated with an accommodation strategy, also prepared by ADP, with the next step being the implementation of the first phases.

The external professional team working with the institution, becomes particularly important in the first reality check around applicability, feasibility, logistics and affordability on the initial options. In the main the applicability question can be determined by consultation within the institution, with an external facilitator who has experience across the particular sector, if such a resource is not available internally.

Leadership on feasibility usually falls on the external design team, supported by the local technical estates, IT and learning and teaching resources. What needs to be determined here is the size and mix of new build, refurbishment, demolition and disposal across the institution and the proposed location of each element, alongside their physical and infrastructural connectivity.

Logistics is important from two standpoints. Firstly, are the components of the plan in the best physical location in order to provide the required benefits? Secondly, how can the plan actually be implemented with regard to phasing, decant and campus movements while the institution remains operational? Here it is necessary that the institution's community are involved along with estates, IT and the external team.

External cost consultants, working alongside the design team, will provide initial estimates of costs for the individual components, proposed phases, and overall implementation of the options. Internal finance experts need to be involved in this process in order to ensure affordability and to co-ordinate with the institution's finance strategy.

The components of this reality check need to be co-ordinated by the estates masterplanning team. The result will be a set of sufficiently detailed options and option appraisals that can be presented to the institution's decision-making board. In discussion with the masterplanning team, the board usually rejects some of the options and asks for further work and clarification on others.

An iterative process between the masterplanning team, the institutional stakeholders and the board then takes place until consensus is reached regarding the overall nature of the plan, or possibly plans, that the board would wish to see developed further.

The further development of the estates masterplan leads to a number of outcomes. Firstly there needs to be a detailed discussion regarding the current position of the estate, the reasons for change, what the objectives of the plan are, how the plan co-ordinates and integrates with the other strategic plans of the institution and how the plan makes its contribution towards delivery of the strategic objectives and hence the institutional vision. This is really the 'scene setter' and justification for the plan and can be used both internally and externally to market, promote and support the plan during its implementation.

The plan then usually follows a 'top down' format, starting at the institutional level and presenting overall objectives for the estate. These could be seen as aspirations for the estate which will be delivered by the projects that are defined later in the plan.

A campus masterplan, or set of plans for a multi-campus institution, then follows. These plans set out the proposed layout of each campus and argue this layout in

As part of the process of preparing a masterplan for the University of Sussex, we worked closely with senior management to ensure that the proposals matched the long-term strategy of the University. Diagrams were used to analyse the qualities of the existing site, and phasing diagrams prepared to assist in preparation of financial models. Due to the presence of ten 1960s listed buildings on the campus—the tightest concentration of post-war listed buildings in the country—ADP was also commissioned to prepare a Conservation Plan which identified the significance of these buildings and how their future should be safeguarded.

Opposite left
This plan, part of our analysis of external spaces and movement through the existing campus, shows how one can move either directly or informally through the centre of the site. A formal axial route, surrounded by hard paving, leads from the campus entrance from the railway station, through Falmer House, then Fulton Court, passing through the "tuning forks" before reaching a sequence of courtyards around which the arts facilities are arranged. The grand gesture peters out rather unsatisfactorily, in Arts D and E. Contrasting with this formality, one can choose to take a meandering route, following the valley floor between mature trees, enjoying the landscape setting.

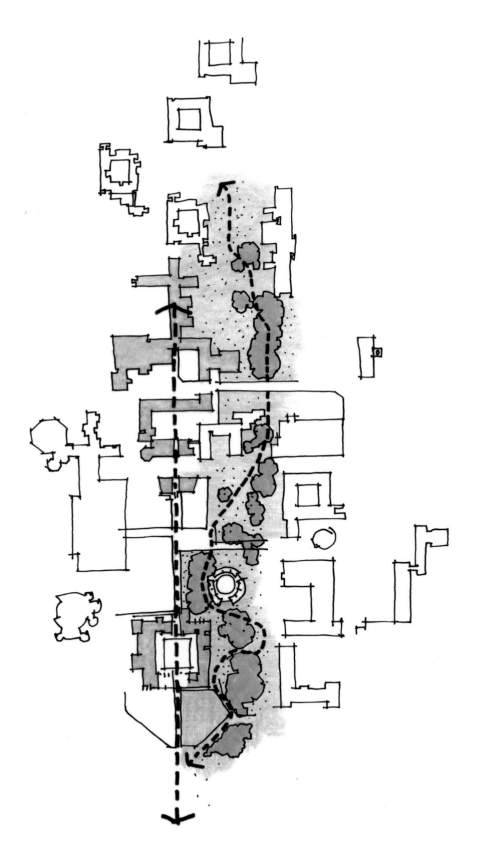

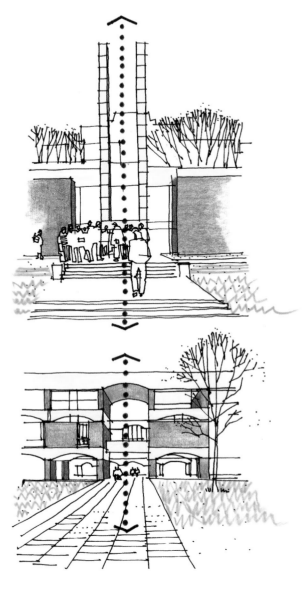

top
The axial route through from Falmer House leads to the great concrete 'tuning fork': a grand and symbolic gesture that announces the entrance to the Arts Buildings.

bottom
Falmer House, a Grade I listed building even though it was only completed in the 1960s, was designed to be the social focus of the campus. It provides the gateway to the pedestrian approach to the University. Organised around a paved quadrangle surrounded by a moat, it leads through to the much larger space of Fulton Court.

terms of strategy, functionality, delivery and logistics. They also consider the individual buildings and the spaces between the buildings in order to discuss the vision and objectives of each component of the plan. They do not go to the level of detailed design; this comes at a later stage when individual parts of the overall plan are developed.

These campus masterplans are particularly useful for consultation with the local authority. Here they can be used to gain outline planning consent for the overall plan, with individual projects then becoming subject to detailed applications within an agreed framework. This can create a positive relationship between the authority and the institution and can avoid major misunderstandings that could subsequently put the institution's strategic development at risk.

This becomes more complex if the masterplan raises more fundamental or strategic issues which may be logical and ultimately acceptable but may not comply with the current local plan, and therefore have to await the next cycle of strategic planning to become formally endorsed.

A section on institutional and campus infrastructure is then usually produced. This moves close to the estates strategy in that it discusses in principle how internal and external environmental objectives are to be achieved and how the general communications and logistic infrastructure will be implemented.

The plan then moves on to phasing, logistics and costing. This breaks down the plan into potential individual projects and indicates how these can be combined into identifiable phases that are logistically feasible, integrate the delivery of strategic objectives and are as self-contained as possible. The major section on costing then defines the estimated cost of each individual project and phase, putting these on time lines defined by the logistics and likely future priorities. This is then rolled up to define the overall costs by time of the plan.

In addition to this, the cost consultants alongside the internal financial team will provide details such as whole-life costings and/or net present value (NPV) calculations to support, or indeed question, the value for money aspects of the masterplan. In fact it is not uncommon for a particular project to be seen as poor value for money given these costing calculations; however other considerations such as profile and reputation or niche market opportunity may well mean it is important that the project be undertaken. The project may be essential to allow expansion in pupil numbers, which generate increased income—which may be needed to fund the project itself in the first place.

Regardless of sector, it is this overall masterplan that needs to be taken to the decision-making board for support and approval. Anything less can lead to uncoordinated and piecemeal development that runs the serious risk of taking a path that is ultimately counterproductive with regard to issues such as academic developments, buildability, affordability, phasing and logistics. It also gives the institution a framework and benchmark within which to evaluate progress and to understand the relationship of the estates masterplan with the other strategic plans.

It is important to recognise, however, that the estates masterplan needs to be a living document, with a medium- to long-term life span. Because of the timescales involved, in large institutions masterplans typically address developments over ranges from six to 20 years, although in some smaller establishments the plan might be delivered over a shorter time.

What is critical is that the masterplan in not 'set in stone', because over the life of the plan circumstances and objectives are inevitably going to change to some degree, be this as a result of external factors such as changes in government policy or internal issues such as essential curriculum developments. It is therefore important that the masterplan is reviewed on a regular basis, typically annually or on the completion of the commissioning of a phase. The normal way of achieving this is to first reconfirm the overall high-level objectives, which should still be appropriate unless the institution or sector has undergone some radical change. The planned phases and individual projects are then considered, in order to establish their continued relevance or to make adjustments as necessary. This process is necessary in order to keep the masterplan relevant and up to date with the requirements of the institution.

Also important with regard to this continual process of reconfirmation and potential readjustment is the ability to consider and respond to unexpected opportunities that might arise from time to time. For example, through an unforeseen external initiative an institution could be approached to host a national centre of excellence, including the creation of a physical facility. Significant but not total funding might be available and space on campus would need to be identified. In this situation an up to date estates masterplan and other strategic plans are invaluable to the institution. An evaluation of the proposal in terms of affordability, academic and business opportunity, physical feasibility, profile and reputation, and institutional infrastructure can readily be undertaken and an informed decision arrived at. Without appropriate institutional planning in place a decision of this nature would be driven by guesswork and could lead to compromises at some later point in time.

While this outline has focused on a large institution to bring out the complexities and issues involved, the themes are still relevant to smaller projects and the process is scaleable to meet the needs of any part of the sector. For example, the involvement of an IT service or an estates department is regularly referred to as part of the design or decision-making process. What is important here is not that such departments exist within the institution, but that an appropriate professional input is available, whether it is from an internal source or elsewhere.

Also, the actual process of decision-making might seem to be convoluted and time consuming. To some extent it needs to be: the issues are fundamental and important and the costs and risks are high, therefore it is necessary to be thorough. But again clearly 'one size fits all' is not appropriate. As long as decisions meet the strategic requirements and cover the critical issues discussed previously, they should ensure that the estate is able to play its full part in the future development of the institution.

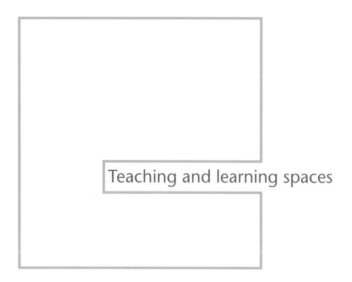

Teaching and learning spaces

Tracing back to the formation of ADP in the 1960s, learning spaces in education were very much as they had been for hundreds of years. The students either sat in rows and listened to a blackboard-supported performance, or they sat in silence in a library and worked alone. They might also conduct experiments in fixed-purpose laboratories, again laid out in rows, and occasionally they might use new technologies to watch a film or television production.

This form of instructional learning had its roots in the religious concept of the preacher and the congregation and although it was, and still is, an efficient method for presenting a message, it does not suit many learning styles.

Over the last 40 years learning and teaching has seen a time of revolution. Pedagogic experience has developed to give understanding of the need to provide different opportunities to suit individual learners. This, coupled with the variety of media by which learning can now be delivered, has led to a recognition that to gain the real benefits from a learning environment, the environment must be designed and created to support not only the teachers and learners but also the learning media.

Understanding these developments while creating flexible and adaptable spaces for the future is a real challenge for the modern designer, not only in the physical design of the spaces themselves but also in the ways that developing technologies can be incorporated.

General teaching and learning spaces have developed from classrooms, where a single session of teaching takes place, into areas where many different sessions can occur in parallel. These spaces abandon the concept of rows of students by using flexible and adaptable interior layouts within technology-rich environments, thereby enabling a variety of learning paradigms to be developed and implemented.

Austere and formal, an architectural expression of rigid teaching methods; classrooms as they used to be.

As these groupings at Collingwood College demonstrate, classrooms can now be laid out quite differently, with computer workstations arranged in small clusters to encourage group working, and the teacher able to circulate easily between groups. Increasing use of flat screens and remote computer hubs reduces the impact of technology still further. Other schools provide laptops to pupils entering the sixth form and allow them to take the computer with them when they leave.

These facilities need to be supplemented by other general spaces such as learning centres, where typically the text-based resource of the institution is housed alongside areas for individual and group learning where there is the availability of a variety of technologies to support the learning process. In a less formal setting the social learning area or internet cafe concept is used to provide a social gathering opportunity within an informal learning environment: drop-in availability of internet-enabled technology is supplemented by a catering offer, alongside a variety of individual and group learning spaces.

Effectiveness and efficiency are concepts that feature high on the agenda when designing facilities for the education sector. Often efficiency is the factor that appears at the top of the list when the vision for a project is created; however what is really required is usually an effective space that can be used efficiently. This is the way to achieving satisfaction and value for money, whereas an efficient space that is ineffective is the way to frustration and waste.

The plan width and floor to floor heights of buildings to house teaching and learning has changed significantly. Many schools and universities now suffer from building stock constructed in the 1950s and 1960s which were built with narrow floorplates and low ceilings. These problems are compounded by inferior external fabric. Whilst the latter can be rectified through being upgraded, the shape of the building is a more fundamental problem. An efficient and flexible modern solution will consist of a central corridor, wide enough to cope with the flow of people at peak times. On either side of this, ideally there will be teaching spaces to accommodate the various group sizes required, ensuring that spaces become neither too narrow (through the space being too deep), nor too long (caused by space which is too shallow). This will give an optimum width of building which will tend to be slightly larger for a university building, accommodating larger teaching groups in seminar rooms, than for a school, housing classrooms on either side of circulation space.

It is important that the learning spaces of an institution provide for the variety of learning and teaching opportunities that enable the learning process to be undertaken in an effective and efficient way. Increasingly, as student needs and pedagogic understanding develop, this process requires support for the 'learn and work anytime, anywhere' paradigm, which of itself implies an approach of flexible, adaptable and sustainable design to the learning facilities.

Teaching and learning spaces clearly differ across the spectrum of education, from primary schools to universities, according to the needs of learners of different ages. In primary schools, education takes place not only through classroom-based teaching but also through creative play. Additional space, such as winter gardens or outdoor spaces attached to classrooms, allow greater flexibility for teachers.

Successfully nurturing children through the difficult transition from pre-school to school is one of the fundamental issues influencing the design and organisation of primary schools. The transfer from pre-school to reception class is a difficult one, and can be assisted by providing consistency in learning methods, familiarity in classroom design and furnishings, mirroring table-top activities and creating opportunities for play and fun.

At Riverhead Infants' School, the Hampshire County Council model of open plan space was considered and eliminated due to concern about noise transmission between teaching spaces: some teachers had had direct experience of teaching in these situations. Instead, classrooms are completely separate, but high-level windows allow some transfer of light, whilst furniture layouts allow for informal groups of pupils. Winter gardens—extra spaces achieved through the efficiency of the plan arrangement—provide additional flexible spaces, for example for "listening to readers", where children read out loud to volunteer parents, outside the classroom environment. Internal windows are positioned at the average eye-height of pupils at the school. Teaching spaces lead outside to formal outdoor learning areas, and to informal play spaces beyond (photos opposite).

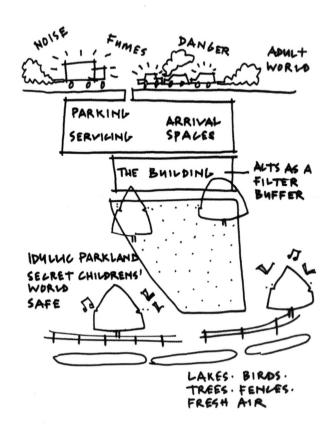

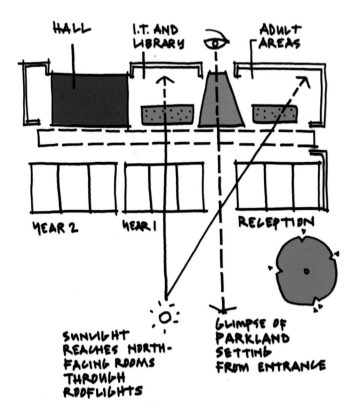

Primary schools should aim to promote children's pride in their environment, and strengthen identity at a time of rapid emotional and psychological growth. Classroom design and teaching methods must also allow for the development in children emotionally, physically and academically, and their progression through personalised learning. This can be done, for example, by giving a sense of progression throughout the school differentiating classrooms for different age pupils using colours. Giving each year of pupils an identity reinforces their educational development.

The transition from primary to secondary is a challenging one for many students. Moving from informal teaching environments to more formal spaces and, by contrast, informal teaching, with a diverse curriculum means many students struggle in their first year. In secondary schools, a current movement in education practice is the "school within a school" model, in which Year 7 pupils have a separate area from the rest of the school. This smoothes the transition from primary into secondary education, which is a major time in pupil development but is intimidating to many. This can be a major influence on parents, when selecting a secondary school—whether state or independent—for their child.

Learning takes place in both informal and more formal ways, and the needs of the school can change over time as teaching methods develop. It is therefore important to incorporate both flexible teaching spaces that could be rearranged if necessary, as well as spaces where pupils learn outside the traditional classroom environment. These spaces would typically be located within, and open to, the circulation space—for example computer clusters within wide corridors.

In developing our approach to the ideal design of a secondary school for part of the government's Building Schools for the Future initiative, we developed a number of studies of the relationship between the main components of the scheme. Key issues include the location of facilities which will be used at times by the local community, such as the main hall, catering and sports facilities, and therefore where the lines of security should be placed. This is a critical aspect, achieving the secure areas required whilst creating an open and welcoming impression.

The layout and distribution of learning spaces is another major decision, balancing separation to create privacy and generous space between building elements with the need to create short and efficient circulation patterns.

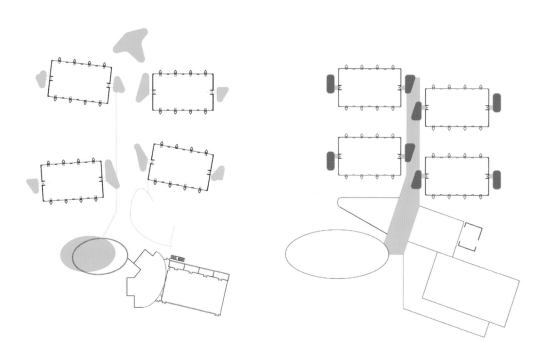

Classrooms can be grouped in different ways—for example by faculty, by year, or by 'house'. And there are some specialist facilities within secondary education—for example science laboratories—which can be located next to generic teaching space for that particular department.

Students' requirements are simple: light, bright and modern spaces which help them to feel relaxed, inspired and comfortable. Governors, trustees and teachers face more challenges: balancing the need for beautiful spaces with requirements for flexibility; user-friendliness; community involvement; ease of maintenance and above all, balancing finances and cost effectiveness, which are more taxing concerns.

The current trend is that teaching and learning spaces in secondary schools will become more open-plan, with flexible spaces that could either be used as larger rooms with small breakout spaces, or subdivided into more traditional classrooms as necessary. This is a strong theme in Building Schools for the Future exemplar schemes.

At the centre of it all, is the community—the 'heart' of the school and the interface between students and the outside world. With increasing focus on the extended school day and the provision of out of school hours learning—for parents as well as for pupils—the need for community-friendly spaces has never been more important.

While future educational changes cannot be fully foreseen, it is necessary to 'future-proof' designs by incorporating a high level of adaptability. The seemingly fastest-moving change in education is the use of Information and Communication Technologies (ICT), and the pace of change is only set to increase into the future. The use of ICT has brought new ways of teaching and learning, and as future generations of pupils will become more advanced users of technology the spaces in which they learn must reflect this. The Building Schools for the Future programme encourages new ways of thinking through a range of exemplar designs which aim to tackle the key social, educational and technological developments that are occurring. These encourage flexibility in the short term, for rearranging spaces to suit different activities, as well as adaptability over the longer term, for example to allow internal walls to be moved to change the size and arrangement of teaching spaces.

In the higher education sector, one of the main reasons for poor space utilisation has been the tendency to design bespoke buildings to suit an immediate research or teaching need. As funding has become increasingly short-term, particularly for research, space designed for the original use frequently becomes redundant. If the cost of converting the existing space is prohibitive, it will result in a new use being put into poorly adapted space and this can significantly reduce the level of utilisation.

A characteristic of higher education in the past has been the tendency to locate teaching accommodation within a well-defined departmental boundary. This can result in space being ring-fenced for that department and consequently running the risk of low levels of utilisation if the department itself uses it infrequently: institutions which have a larger proportion of teaching rooms subject to pooling and central timetabling achieve greater space efficiencies and potential for stimulating dialogue between students and staff studying or teaching different subjects.

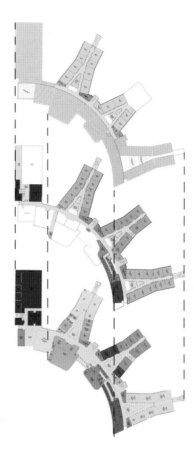

Circulation in schools needs to be right, to create efficient movement of large numbers of pupils at certain times, with good visibility to ensure safety and to minimise opportunities for unsociable behaviour. Circulation spaces can widen out to create zones for learning, whilst the inter-relationship between subject areas is another key factor. Departments need to be able to expand and contract whilst maintaining individual identity; this has to be balanced with ensuring high levels of room occupancy and utilisation—i.e. the room sizes match as closely as possible the pupil numbers occupying the space, and rooms are in use for as much of the working day as possible. This issue is not unique to schools, applying equally to further education colleges and universities.

A number of schools are trying to reduce the amount of circulation by creating year bases. In this model the teacher will move around rather than the pupils, which can be far less disruptive to the school day.

Circulation is vital to the successful operation of teaching and learning spaces. It deals with the efficient and safe movement of students, but also contributes to the overall ambience. At St Olave's Grammar School, we have designed functional and flexible areas for teaching music and science, and for sixth form learning and recreation.

As important as these useable spaces are the external courtyards and the circulation spaces. We have used the new buildings to create new quadrangles, continuing the theme of the original layout. Double height spaces create accent and a sense of space at building entrances and to main circulation areas, whilst attractively detailed staircases ensure easy movement between floor levels. Internal walls are picked out in the School's distinctive colours. A tight budget has been carefully allocated to ensure that the building conveys a positive impression through its circulation, and formal teaching and learning spaces operate effectively.

In order to be sustainable, specialist spaces also need to exhibit flexibility and adaptability wherever possible. For example, the single-specialism science laboratory has been replaced by areas where a variety of cognate topics can be explored in an effective and efficient way, thereby enabling education to sustain critical areas of curriculum in a climate of falling specialist numbers. Studio spaces for subjects such as performing arts, design and media production can be expensive to produce and therefore need to be efficient to use while remaining effective and providing good value for money. Typically the requirement is for flexibility and adaptability in order to sustain a major investment.

Information Technology is something of a hybrid in terms of specialist learning and teaching spaces. In the early days of computing education the computing students tended to be the ones who monopolised the facilities in order to explore computer science. Although these students still have this requirement, the majority access in an institution is now in the use of computers to engage with other subjects and as the major communication tool. This creates a requirement for specialist spaces, such as network and real-time laboratories, plus bookable and open access areas, which can be used by specialists and non-specialists alike. Future-proofing these facilities in a climate of perpetual technological development and change is a major design issue.

ADP has developed a detailed masterplan for the phased development of the Medical School at the University of Birmingham. This strategy rationalises the main circulation flow through the existing building, converts existing space to new uses, and allows for the addition of new accommodation.

New learning areas have been inserted into the existing building (below).

The front entrance to the new School of
Sport and Exercise and Science, for the
University of Birmingham, which contains
a variety of both specialist and general
teaching and learning spaces.

The new School of Sport and Exercise Science for the University of Birmingham (Sportex) required a range of different teaching and learning spaces. These were grouped according to their requirements and expressed in the completed project. Specialist timber-clad lecture theatres have bespoke requirements and form sculptural shapes that provide a focus to the composition. Specialist laboratories with high servicing requirements demand high ceilings and closely controlled environmental conditions which are expressed in a purpose-built new wing. Smaller cellular accommodation such as offices have been housed in an upgraded existing building. As important as the formal accommodation requirements, the circulation areas are critical to the success of a building such as this, with a naturally lit and generous atrium forming the heart of the complex: a venue for informal exchange of ideas and theories that emerge when 'breaking-out' from formal research sessions.

Auditoria

Large scale auditoria are often seen as the centrepiece of a campus, providing a measure of gravitas and status. However, the requirement for these auditoria to provide space for large lectures is supplemented by a need for flexibility of use and often of opportunity to integrate with the local community or to generate external revenue. Given the expense of providing these facilities it is not surprising that institutions tend to take the attitude that the space should earn its keep. Therefore, although it may be difficult to make an auditorium adaptable, they are often required to be flexible enough to cater not only for large lectures but also for high profile presentations, concerts, dramatic performances, conferences and possibly even exhibitions.

Central to the traditional delivery of teaching in higher education has been the lecture theatre or auditorium. The delivery of lectures to a captured audience of students or an invited group of guests has long been the centrepiece of a didactic form of teaching. Although styles of teaching and learning have become considerably more varied, particularly with the development of information technology, the need to deliver set-piece lectures remains an important part of the academic calendar. Auditoria are either located within a departmental boundary or are arranged as a central campus facility, available to all. This choice of how to provide the facilities reveals one of the central dilemmas in the optimisation of auditorium design. The knowledge of how a lecture theatre is to be used is essential in ensuring the ultimate success of the building and a design optimised for one subject may well be inappropriate in a number of ways for another.

The style of teaching of the subject can have a significant effect on the form of the auditorium. For instance teaching in business schools tends to be highly interactive with the audience. The lecturer wishes to have a dialogue with the audience and to promote discussion amongst the students. Therefore the form of the lecture theatre should result in a relatively short distance from the lecturer to the back seat in theatre; the layout of seats should be curved so that members of the audience can see each other and the area at the front should be large to allow the lecturer to move around.

A carefully formulated curved seating plan and gentle rake provides Aston Business School with a desirable relationship between speaker and audience. Generous upholstered seating and acoustic treatment to the rest of the auditorium ensures the comfort of the users.

The teaching wall should be large to allow a number of types of visual aid to be used. In its most extreme form the layout becomes a horseshoe, as pioneered by the Harvard Business School. Although this form works best for smaller groups of around 40 it can be adapted for a larger cohort, as demonstrated in ADP's two lecture theatres at the Aston Business School.

Harvard Business School, showing shape and rake of seating. Note the curved plan forms and angle of rake to the seating areas, allowing for audience participation.

The physicists who would be using the lecture theatre designed by ADP at University of Oxford calculated the length of the longest equation they would need to write: this was used to establish the necessary size of the blackboard.

By way of contrast the lecture theatre at the Department of Physics at the University of Oxford was optimised for the teaching of that subject. A significant characteristic of this style of teaching, common to mathematics, is the extensive use of blackboards. Although this teaching aid has been around for many years, and is absent from many modern lecture theatres, it remains the best way for a lecturer to display a long, complex and developing mathematical argument, consequently the teaching wall needs not only to be wide but also tall. In addition the display of live physical experiments on a table at the front of the lecture theatre dictated that the rake of the seats needed to be steep to allow the audience to look down onto the table. This also meant that the viewing angle of the large blackboards could be improved. Consequently it can be seen that for some auditoria the content of the course being taught can affect the design.

Another significant factor is the size of the anticipated audience. Large lecture theatres with more than 250 seats have been relatively rare in recent years because it was perceived that the number of courses that could justify a large seating capacity were relatively few. A large lecture theatre would have a relatively low level of utilisation as most audiences were a poor fit for the seats available and two smaller lecture theatres with the total capacity of the larger alternative offered a more flexible solution, even allowing for a lecture to be given in one theatre whilst being simultaneously broadcast to an overflow audience located elsewhere. Occasionally an opportunity for a larger lecture theatre does arise if a course has a particularly large intake and has significant lecture based content. Medical schools can have a large undergraduate intake and frequently combine first- and second-year teaching with related subjects such as biomedical sciences and dentistry, creating a substantial cohort that can be taught simultaneously.

The lecture theatre at the University of Birmingham Medical School was designed for a combined cohort of 450 students and was optimised for the teaching of medicine. The characteristics of larger lecture theatres include the increased importance of acoustics to ensure that the lecturer remains audible in all parts of the auditorium. At Birmingham sound reinforcement has been provided, however the acoustics are so good that it can function most of the time with this switched off. Access to the lecture theatre is important and students should be able to enter the space after the lecture has started without causing significant distraction to the lecturer. At Birmingham this is achieved by having entrances at the lowest level supplemented by additional doors at mid-level. The activity within the auditorium is visible on a video screen at the entrance allowing the student to choose the most discrete point of entry. Large auditoria can be soulless so a careful consideration of room shape and seating rake should take place to ensure that the space remains as intimate as possible and the student and lecturer remain in contact.

The size of the adjacent spaces needs to be given a lot of thought particularly when an auditorium is part of a central teaching complex. When lectures change on the hour, the surrounding circulation space can become very crowded with students entering and leaving different auditoria. If auditoria have been designed around a linking street or concourse this needs to be large enough to cope with peak traffic flows. Careful consideration needs to be given to these spaces which at other times could be wasted and the introduction of exhibition space and social activities can give them more purpose and increase space efficiency.

The need for exhibition space is doubly important if it is intended that the auditorium will also be used for conferences; either for academic purposes or commercial lettings. An auditorium can bring considerable status to an institution if it is associated with high quality conference activities. However it is important that if this is the intention the auditorium is of a sufficiently high quality to attract conference organisers who have a multiplicity of choices. The quality of the auditorium needs to be considered in detail, including, for instance, factors such as seat comfort. A seat that might be comfortable for an undergraduate attending a one hour lecture may well be inadequate for a delegate attending a day long conference. Audio visual equipment needs to be of the highest quality yet easy to use by a conference speaker who is unfamiliar with it. Ancillary spaces need to be large enough to provide conference delegates with refreshments, or even to feed them at lunch time, and toilets need to be close by and sized to take the peak demand in breaks.

There were concerns that the large size of the lecture theatre at the University of Birmingham Medical School could be intimidating for lecturers, and that it would be too large to hold the attention of students in the back seats. However, by careful consideration of plan form and rake of seating, the size of the space and audience has been disguised. The resulting intimate space has caused several visitors to count the seats to confirm that it really is a 450-seat auditorium.

The potentially rigid form of the auditoria can make them the enemy of space efficiency and there have been many attempts to increase their flexibility both in terms of size and use. Devices used include moveable walls, retractable seating and variable acoustics. The success of these will be largely determined by the principal use of the space. If this is a well-defined and frequent use and its functionality is compromised in order to make it usable for secondary, infrequent purposes then there is the danger that the design will be viewed as a failure for all functions. If the effort required to adapt a space is significant then there is the possibility that the intended flexibility will rarely be used as the labour required to adapt the space is seldom available. The key to determining the appropriate level of flexibility is a good dialogue with the client and developing an understanding of how the space will be used. The design should avoid providing flexibility where there is no demonstrable need as this is likely to waste money, but where a multi-use can be defined then appropriate measures can be taken. Perhaps the most useful flexibility is provided by retractable seating, allowing a raked floor to be replaced with a flat floor. At the School of Art, Design and Technology at the University of Derby four auditoria have been provided with retractable seating allowing the spaces to be used as lecture halls, drama studios, lighting studios and examination halls.

At the University of Surrey four lecture theatres announce their presence behind a brick facade through the use of bold colour, modern art and confident graphics. One 400-seat and one 300-seat auditorium can be subdivided to create two 200-seat and two 150-seat spaces respectively, with a high-performance acoustic wall separating the spaces. Seating can be retracted to create flat-floor areas suitable for open days, exhibitions, and spaces for examinations. One space has a carpet floor whilst the other has a semi-sprung floor for dance. Associated storage areas were provided; it is vital that if a variety of functions are to be accommodated, space is allowed for the necessary furniture and equipment to support those other uses.

The most difficult flexibility to achieve is to design an auditorium for both speech and music. The short reverberation times required for clear audible speech are inappropriate for music. In smaller auditoria it is difficult to achieve the acoustic conditions suitable for listening to music. Although it is possible to adjust the acoustic performance of an auditorium it is seldom cost effective in a Higher Education environment where the music component is always likely to be subordinate to speech.

The large volume and height of an auditorium and the limited requirement for windows makes them a useful element in the architectural palette for creating dramatic statements, and lecture theatres are frequently used to create centrepieces in a composition. They can be used externally to give a form and shape to a facade or to denote entrances, or can be used as elements within the building to create dynamic forms around which space can be arranged.

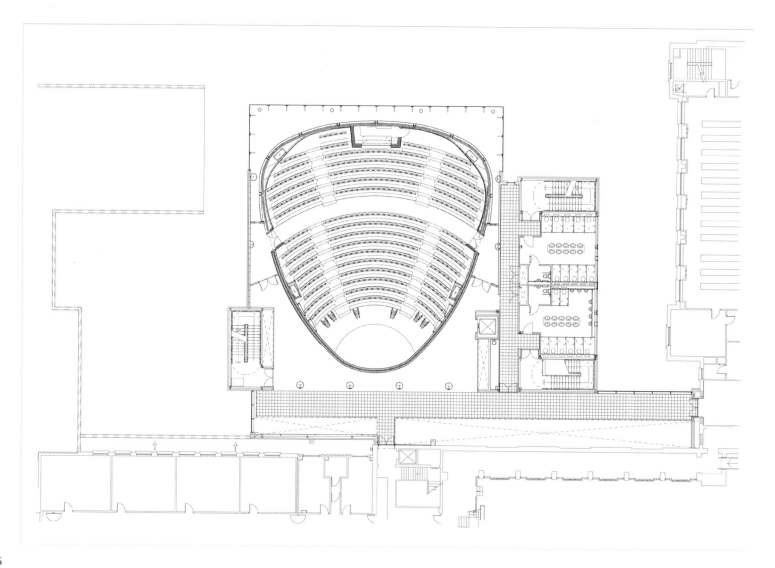

The lecture theatre at the Medical School at the University of Birmingham takes the form of a timber clad egg hovering within a four storey space under which is arranged the student social and refectory.

The conceptual form of this lecture theatre is that of an 'egg in a box', but the precise layout is also the result of exhaustive studies to find the optimum shape to meet its functional requirements, notably the need for excellent acoustics for speech to an audience of 450.

At Aston Business School the two lecture theatres are contrasting dynamic forms sitting within a double-height gallery space. In both cases the auditoria are used to create impressive spaces that raise the profile of the institution and have a positive effect on visitors to the buildings.

Spaces for living

The changing needs for living spaces in education reflect the differences between accommodation for different sectors of the education market—including Higher Education (undergraduate and postgraduate), Oxbridge colleges, boarding schools, management colleges and associated conference facilities.

Designers of student accommodation are faced with the challenge of creating environments that are conducive to both social life and study. The process of design is in equal parts an architectural and social exercise: for many students, the accommodation will be their first time away from their parental home and the social interactions that are encouraged (or discouraged) will form an important part of school or university life.

The needs of social groupings and shared facilities must be addressed alongside effectiveness of building form: the arrangement and grouping of student rooms can have an important impact on the students' sense of security and belonging. An understanding of human psychology is required. The arrangement of individual rooms and communal facilities can encourage the formation of functional social units where groups of students will take ownership and responsibility of an area, and exercise an element of self-governance over each other. This has advantages of improving both the perceived and actual security and a reduction of damage in use.

The optimum number of students to group together in a unit will vary depending on age, experience, type of institution level of study, etc. As a generalisation young undergraduates living away from home for the first time can benefit from larger groups of up to say eight (however this must be balanced with behavioural problems that can be caused by larger groupings) whereas more mature graduates are suited to groups of six or less.

Good student accommodation must fulfil a number of important criteria: providing attractive, high quality living accommodation, economic operation and low energy design; utilising robust, attractive and low maintenance materials, finishes and fittings which are easy to repair; and in many cases, fulfil stringent sustainability criteria as well. In the case of the University of Bath issues of life-cycle costing and a commitment to effective environmental management strategies have been met head on, significantly influencing design development. Concrete panel construction was chosen for robustness, thermal mass, acoustic properties and speed of construction. The building itself, 'steps down' towards the boundary of the site, while the 'E' formation allows for effective integration of landscape design.

The building will provide 355 units of undergraduate and postgraduate accommodation and is located on the edge of the existing campus, adjacent to an Area of Outstanding Natural Beauty.

The design of this project for the University of Bath combines three key factors. The response to the site is described later in Contextualism and the sustainable aspects are outlined in the chapter on sustainability. The functional requirement of the building is primarily derived from the repetition of study bedrooms, and the shared communal areas including the means of circulation.

The ideal layout allows the option of access to all bedrooms via a lift, and this has been achieved by grouping flats of up to 15 students around a lift at one core and a staircase at another. A typical arrangement is shown below, but this layout has been varied within the scheme to accommodate variations in the site, to respond to differing orientation of the blocks, and to integrate postgraduate accommodation. These factors introduce opportunities to change the basic arrangement, thereby providing a logical variation and human scale to the most efficient layout.

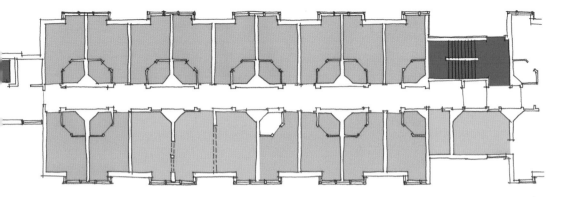

STUDY BEDROOM

COMMUNAL LIVING + DINING

VERTICAL CIRCULATION

Large open dormitories are no longer suitable for boarding schools. Here, the social groupings reflect a critical phase in development from child to adult. Typically, pupils will initially be in larger groups of eight per room, which may be subdivided into smaller areas but with a large shared space. By Year 9 the groups might reduce to four, and by Years 10 and 11 pupils might share a room with one other. In the Sixth Form, Years 12 and 13 may have their own rooms; this grouping might have their own accommodation block separate from the younger pupils. Older pupils may have small en-suite facilities—not only to provide privacy but also so that accommodation can be let to other users during vacation periods.

Christ's Hospital Foundation, founded by Edward VI in 1552, is a unique institution, the largest educational charity in the country, with a vast endowment. Many great schools were established to educate the poor, but Christ's Hospital is unique in the extent to which it has been able to carry on that tradition.

When it moved out from the City of London to a 1,200 acre site close to Horsham in 1902, Sir Aston Webb won a competition to design new facilities. These included large open dormitories with sanitary facilities at the end. ADP won a competition to reconfigure all the boarding house accommodation to meet modern spatial and technical standards and expectations. A phased refurbishment began in 1999 and this vast task is due to be completed in 2008. Pupils will benefit from increased social areas, improved sanitary facilities, and a graduation from larger to smaller bedroom groupings as they progress through the school (left and below).

Within the rather solemn original Aston Webb boarding houses, traditional layouts and furnishings have been replaced by modern arrangements and bright, colourful interiors.

The range of types of student accommodation varies, from the collegiate halls of Oxbridge colleges to the dormitories of many independent schools, to small-scale blocks of 'flats' and large dense blocks (either vertically or horizontally linear) of rooms in a 'hotel' format.

Within large blocks of rooms, there will be shared facilities for students such as dining, laundry, and recreation. Either tall, with circulation by stairs or lift, or wide, with circulation by long corridors, this model allows effectiveness of circulation space. However the penalty is the creation of an 'institutional' feel, and the loss of character and belonging which is inherent in smaller-scale halls.

Small 'flats' in blocks from a central core (up to around four storeys) will lead to reduced effectiveness of vertical circulation but will create small 'family' social groupings of students sharing a kitchen and dining area.

Student accommodation facilities must balance public and private space: the shared facilities are important for building community but equally important is the private study bedroom. To meet cost targets it is usually necessary for individual rooms to be kept to simple, repetitive rectangular form. Within this simple framework value can be added by maximising space utilisation and enhancing the users' experience. Subtleties in room design can have a strong effect on the users' perception of the space, their sense of security and enjoyment of a space. Many of these issues involve refinement in the configuration of standard room components that will add value without additional cost.

At Christ's Hospital (this page and previous) the magnificence and grandeur of the setting provide a traditional environment for the pupils, reinforced by the uniform and customs of the School. ADP has prepared a masterplan for the whole site, exploiting its history whilst creating opportunities for the future.

The requirements of boarding house accommodation can be 'read' from this elevation, a photograph of St Edward's School in Oxford. On the left, a private house for the houseparent. Frequently, a houseparent today will be married and with children, so the expectation is that a good quality house with a number of bedrooms and its own private garden, will be provided. Typically, this links through a study to the boarding accommodation.

Pupils generally start in larger rooms, typically for four pupils, before graduating to a shared room and ultimately their own single room. The size and specification of this will often at least match the quality now being offered in University Halls of Residence. Communal areas are provided to give social and recreational areas, as well as spaces for private study.

STUDY BEDROOM
COMMUNAL LIVING + DINING
VERTICAL CIRCULATION

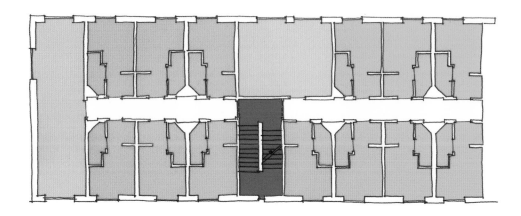

STUDY-BEDROOM
VERTICAL CIRCULATION
GATEHOUSE

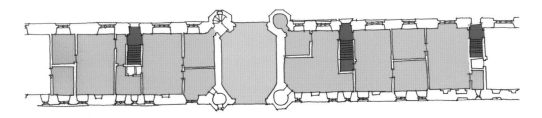

top
The plan above is a typical part-floor plan of our design to provide the University of Sussex with 232 new study bedrooms. The layout is broadly modelled on the Oxbridge staircase layout, with groups of study bedrooms arranged around the vertical circulation. Typically, there are flats of six and seven bedrooms on either side of a staircase, on three levels. This creates a series of group sizes to which the student can relate: a small group which together forms a flat and which shares a kitchen and living area: six or seven is an ideal size, large enough to find a friend, but not so large as to be overwhelming.

There will also be opportunities for occasional contact with others on the same floor served by the same staircase: here the group size is typically 13. There will also be the chance of meeting others using the same staircase: the group size here becomes 39.

The layout is essentially three similar parallel blocks, each accommodating around 78 students, so there are further larger groupings of 78 and the size of the whole scheme, 232. The rooms are clustered around two quadrangles, giving an identity to the whole group. There are therefore a series of groupings—six or seven, 13, 39, 78 and 232—with matching architectural expression—flat, floor level, staircase, building and courtyard.

bottom
The layout of the University of Sussex project can be compared and contrasted with the arrangement (left) which shows a traditional Oxford or Cambridge College, (in this case, Trinity College in Cambridge). Here, individual rooms are arranged on either side of a staircase which leads directly up from the quadrangle. Rooms or sets were divided into a study and bedroom, often now adapted to include a small bathroom. Rooms occupy the full width of the building, which is of domestic scale and construction, whereas for the University of Sussex scheme many more rooms are served by each staircase, 'double-banked' on either side of a central corridor. The fundamental principle, of creating small groups on either side of the vertical circulation is the same, and contrasts with the the 1960s pattern of layout, where many more study bedrooms were arranged along long narrow corridors. Whilst this achieved greater numbers of rooms for every staircase, with a long and institutional corridor it is more difficult to create smaller and supportive groups of students.

Important considerations include placement of the bed—the privacy given by the room can be improved by screening the bed from the opening door and placing the headboard in a strong 'defensible' location with a view of the approach from the door. Differentiating areas within the bedroom by creating distinct sleeping area and workspace, with a 'service area' of en-suite and storage by the door, encourages separation of relaxation time and study time. The size and placement of windows has a critical effect on the sense of enclosure, natural lighting, security and connection with the outside. A vital element is the provision for appropriation of the space by the occupant: pinboards and picture rails allow them to claim the space with their own graphics and decorations, without damaging the internal finishes. Each academic year, rooms will have a new occupant and therefore internal finishes must be robust. It will be necessary to undertake regular maintenance and decoration, but steps should be taken to reduce the need for this.

It is a standard requirement to include en-suite facilities in modern accommodation, as students will expect this. In the past, such facilities were not standard and therefore a common challenge for designers is refurbishing and modernising existing accommodation to meet current expectations.

The layout of the study bedrooms in relation to the circulation and social areas is vital. The traditional Oxbridge layout places study bedrooms on either side of a staircase, and the student identifies with the stair and quadrangle in which they live. Dining in the Great Hall is an opportunity to bring the collegiate community together. These traditions, however, are being eroded: the staircase layout as described is inefficient and students today have both the wealth and inclination to make their own arrangements for catering, rather than sharing a communal occasion.

Accessibility has become prevalent in all areas of life, and is an important consideration in designing spaces for living. Opportunities for the designer include specifying the ground floor for disabled users (to minimise the need for lift access to upper floors) or those with disabled family members likely to visit. Student accommodation must provide a safe and secure environment. Security can be incorporated into the design, by designing out opportunities for crime—straightforward methods include combining unobtrusive physical security with well-tested principles of natural surveillance and defensible space. By careful design, security can be incorporated without compromising the quality of the environment.

The construction of new student accommodation represents a very significant investment which can only be embarked upon with assurance that the income revenue stream can be maintained over a considerable period of time. One aspect of reducing the long-term risk is to ensure that the building could be occupied by a range of users; it is important to ensure that the building could be adapted for alternative users at minimal cost. For example, university halls of residence can be rented to the conference market during academic holidays.

The success of this, and a major part of students' selection criteria, will depend on the other facilities being offered as part of the overall 'student experience'. Social, recreational and leisure facilities will support the living accommodation and make a key contribution to student life.

This scheme for the University of Oxford provides modern and attractive swimming facilities. The quality of leisure, recreational and social facilities, in support of living, learning and teaching accommodation are key ingredients to the student experience of a Higher Education institution.

E-Learning

E-learning started back in the 1960s with developments such as the Dartmouth Time Sharing System and the invention of the language BASIC at Dartmouth College, New Hampshire, USA by Tom Kurtz and John Kemeny, and in the UK by schools' programmes led by people such as Doug Toose. These initiatives were based around paper tape, using machine code or an 'autocode', with peripheral hardware the size of a large filing cabinet to transmit programmes down telephone lines between schools and hosting centres in colleges. They were a far cry from what we now recognise as everyday facilities, however the concepts of the pioneers were far-sighted and outweighed the power of technology to deliver.

Like many other areas of technological development, e-learning visionaries spent over 20 years trying to make a real impact. As is often the case, this was an application waiting for technology to catch up. What made the transformation were developments such as the Internet and the World Wide Web, the increasing bandwidth of internal and external networks, the enhanced power of the desktop computer and the creation of Virtual Learning Environments, for example Lotus Learning Space and the Apple Classroom of Tomorrow.

These developments, and many others, have led to the situation we experience today, where in the developed world the majority of time spent on formal learning is undertaken either directly using or supported by technology. The transformation has been rapid and its effects on education, training and the business and commercial communities have been dramatic. Important in these changes are the way that we design for and incorporate these technologies within the facilities where we work and learn, not only for today but to create sustainability and resilience for the future.

In the context of an educational establishment, some 15 to 20 years ago the business-critical central systems would probably have been seen as some form of student recording system, the order processing system and the payroll system. These were all transaction processing systems, capable of working in a batch processing mode and not really requiring any significant real-time capability. This meant that institutions

Students today are totally familiar with the use of computers as a source of information, for preparing designs, developing documents and presentations, and as a means of communication. For example, pupils at the Centre of Vocational Excellence in Ealing interchange between use of computers with traditional drawing techniques to develop design ideas. It is essential that the building provides a setting that supports and encourages dynamic teaching and learning environments, and is able to integrate constantly changing technology.

could work effectively with a computer service running the business from a central facility. Academic PCs were then generally used for stand-alone work and could be connected to large servers by dedicated networks. These large servers were perhaps then linked or connected to a Wide Area Network such as the embryonic JANET (Joint Academic Network).

What we now have is very different. The mission-critical systems are typically the virtual learning environment, e-mail, the student management system and Internet access. All of these systems are real-time and require fast, resilient network access and filestores. The implication of this for the present and the future are immense, not only in the implementation of institutional infrastructure, but also for the design of the physical environment in order to support future developments.

These internal studies for the new Learning Centre for Canterbury Christ Church University demonstrate how libraries are now seen as far more dynamic spaces, offering a wide range of options, from quiet zones with individual study booths, to opportunities for group working around computer clusters. Different media are used, from traditional books to modern technology. Acoustics are a vital issue, ensuring that users can use the different types of space in the ways intended. Flexibility to adapt to meet future requirements is critical and it is certain that layouts will change over the life of the building; devices such as shapely walls and strong colours are then needed to create a sense of place, clear circulation routes and ability to find one's way around the building.

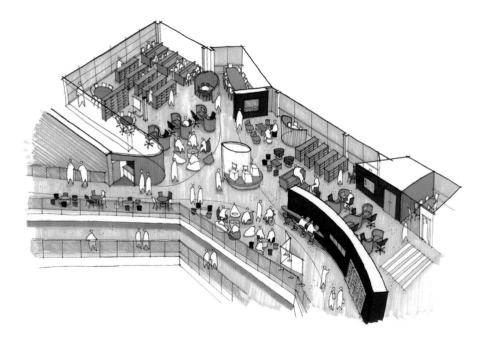

The physical e-learning environment itself takes many forms. Typically there will be the IT classroom or laboratory which is the direct descendent of the early designs. These spaces are generally used for timetabled access and therefore in the 'teaching of students' situation. What is disturbing here is that often these facilities are still produced using serried ranks of computers, all facing the instructor or facing the walls. This makes meaningful interaction difficult as the teacher or the students are unable to really see what is going on, physical involvement of the teacher is difficult and real group working is impossible. In this case pedagogic thinking has not moved in 40 years. Different pedagogically driven layouts are now being successfully implemented which allow structured working, meaningful teacher interaction and group work. These layouts tend to use the concept of the multiple station learning 'pod' and provide a more conducive environment based around differing angles and shapes. Informal drop-in spaces, social learning areas and Internet cafes tend to use the pod and social lounge idea more freely, although it is not unusual to encounter lines of machines facing solid walls, which is isolating for many people. Formal areas in learning centres are the one space where ranks of computers are generally appropriate. Here students are expected to work on their own and to be quiet, so the serried rank concept, while not being attractive, does provide an effective environment.

E-learning itself tends to be based around the Virtual Learning Environment as a harness and using electronic information sources such as the Internet and digital libraries to support content access and creation. The Virtual Learning Environment then provides the framework through which the student works in an e-Learning mode in order to progress their studies.

This implies the design of a major, resilient network across the institution and the provision of this network capability to the desktop or laptop. Here a sophisticated design, involving some mechanical and electrical work to ensure appropriate power and environmental control, network capability and resilience, is required. Alongside this are needed facilities such as Voice over Internet Protocol (VoIP) telephony to provide flexibility, wireless capability to support the learn/work anywhere paradigm, and Storage Area Networks with back-up server facilities to create filestore and business resilience.

Requirements such as these necessitate a co-ordination and integration of technologies in the physical design of the facility or the institution. Essentially these requirements are driven by the need to implement an environment that incorporates e-learning at is centre. However, they also provide the potential for further benefits to be derived for the institution. For example, the network and Internet Protocol (IP) technologies enable physical control systems to be monitored and controlled from a central point. Alongside this, features such as smart card access control, CCTV and other security systems can be implemented as a by-product: all of this leading to the concept of 'intelligent' estates and further to 'intelligent' institutions.

E-learning taxes the designer's skills across a wide and often unexpected spectrum of issues. These range from the highly visible and fundamental design of spaces where e-learning can take place, through to the hidden physical infrastructure that provides the enabling mechanism and the opportunity for sustainability. Modern technology is constantly evolving, directly affecting how buildings are used. Coupled with the impact of sustainable design issues, which we discuss in the final section of the book, design responses are still emerging as we seek optimum solutions to these influences.

Much of ADP's current work, and that over the past 40 years, has been in sensitive settings, and our philosophy in terms of how to approach such challenges is a third major influence on how design solutions develop. We discuss this approach in the next chapter.

At Brunel University, in conjunction with improved 1960s lectures theatres and circulation spaces, new drop-in open access computer areas provide e-learning facilities for students, directly accessed off main pedestrian routes.

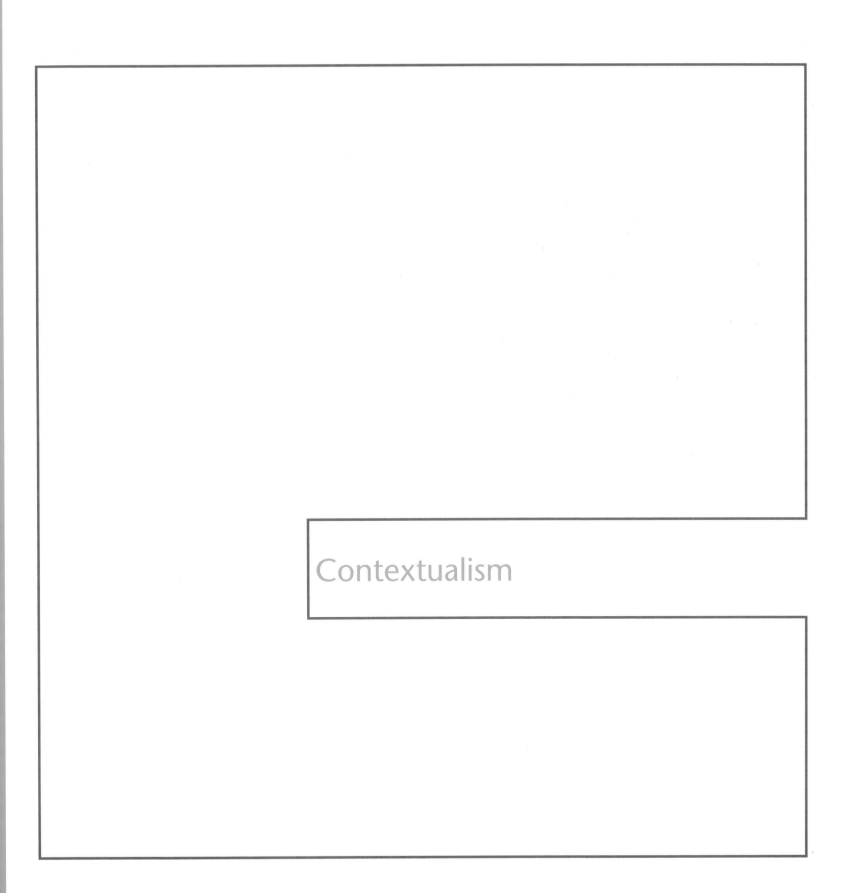

Contextualism

As outlined in the opening pages, Architects Design Partnership's design approach is bespoke, tailoring solutions to suit the specific needs of our clients and responding directly to the physical setting in which the new form is to be built.

In this chapter we explore this approach, founded on analysis and a response to context. We begin by considering the philosophical definition of this approach, before reviewing it at various scales: from the context of a whole region to the detail of materials that are used locally; from the influence of a broad urban setting to the impact of an adjoining listed building.

We then review the significance of contextualism in architectural theory: through history, some buildings have blended seamlessly with their surrounds, whilst many others have been imposed upon them. Today, with the imperative that we design responsible buildings that minimise their environmental impact, comes a new view of what contextualism means… which links into the final chapter.

Philosophy—What is contextualism?

Contextualism is "a doctrine which emphasises the importance of the context of enquiry in a particular question". Architects Design Partnership's approach to design takes account of the context in which we are designing, arriving at solutions through a logical process that is based on thorough analysis and understanding of client needs, and sensitive appraisal of the setting in which the architecture will be found. The context is "the circumstances that form the setting for an event, statement or idea, and in terms of which it can be fully understood" (Oxford Dictionary of English). In the case of architecture the "event, statement or idea" is a building, and "circumstances" that surround it range from the social, political, cultural and economic environment in which it is built, as well as the more obvious physical setting. The origin of the word is from Latin *contextus,* from *con-* "together" and *texere-* "to weave". These words reflect rather well our philosophy: our approach is prepared in unison with those who employ us, and our buildings are weaved into their surroundings, so that they become an integral part of them.

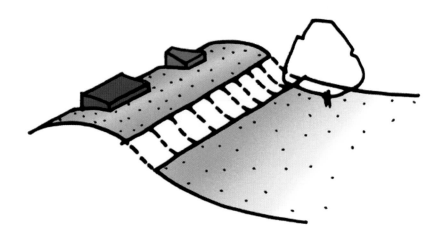

Where does this approach sit in relation to current thinking in the profession at the moment—the architectural context in which we work? Perfectly comfortably. There is a place for the special and iconic design, the attention-seeker. However, we would caution that there can only be so many attention-seekers and that a few moments of fame and publicity for a building need to be coupled in the long term by functionality and durability. At the other extreme, there is a place for the most careful and sensitive restoration of historic fabric, where the architect's input involves the lightest touch, a moment of care in the long history of a special building. Our place, on the whole, is in the mainstream between these two positions. Generalising, our work is not iconic and the instructions we receive do not warrant this. Equally, it is rare that we are asked to undertake purely specialist restoration work. In the main, our commissions are to provide functional buildings that enhance their settings. A contextual approach, derived through logical and careful analysis, matches that requirement very well.

This early concept sketch of Riverhead Infants' School shows how the parkland context and new building were integrated with each other. The red entrance and blue communal hall were expressed as strong geometric shapes.

In the other arts, contextualism has a different and more limited meaning. The creation of a painting or a piece of music, for example, has a context, but that is more usually to do with the artistic context in which something new has been created: what other artists were painting at the time; what other composers were producing. These works are produced in a wider context, that of society, which creates demand and interest in artistic endeavour: where work is commissioned it is a direct response to that need, whilst speculative creations are free of that restraint and can be prepared in a greater spirit of isolation or innovation.

A new context has been created at the railway station end of the University of Birmingham, West Campus, forming a sense of place and arrival for the pedestrian travelling by public transport. Modern new buildings have been positioned and shaped to reinforce a main axis towards the Sir Aston Webb clocktower, and to create a new urban space with a statue by Sir Eduardo Paolozzi acting as the focal point.

In a broader interpretation than just the physical environment, context may also apply to the wider social, political, historical and philosophical backdrop within which we work. As we outlined in section one, ADP's approach to providing an architectural service is to ensure that we identify our client's aspirations and what they wish to achieve from a building project. Helping an institution to achieve its broad strategy and objectives is 'contextual' in the sense that the building reinforces the client's aims and mission through the language of architecture. In turn, we then help shape the future image of the institution through new architecture, which then forms part of the context for future building projects. In science or philosophy, new thinking is produced in a context, that of existing theories and evidence. Again, this is a rather narrow definition. In terms of physical context, we shape our surroundings through landscaping and agricultural projects, through major engineering schemes, and by creating built form. Applied to architecture, the context in which we work is most obviously the physical environment. A design that is contextual does not necessarily blend with its surroundings, but if it represents a contrast it does so deliberately. It is a matter of judgement as to what is the appropriate response to suit a particular context. This requires a degree of flexibility and mental dexterity. Sometimes a deferential or even subservient approach will be appropriate; the opposite extreme would be provocative and iconic but this may be no less suitable. Between these extremities lie a host of solutions which are subtle rather than assertive; which respect history but are not bound by it, which enjoy and even celebrate the challenge of designing to suit an important context.

Through our contextual design approach we can help to educate those who use and see a building. The messages being conveyed, either directly or indirectly, include respect for the environment, sensitivity for the setting, and architecture acts as a logical provider of user needs. If this all seems rather responsive and unambitious, of course there is an aim to delight as well.

In later parts of this section we will describe what we mean by contextual design in different situations, from urban to rural settings, in townscapes and streetscenes, where near or within listed buildings, and at varying scales from the regional context to the use of detail.

A significant factor in the way we design is the influence of current thinking in the architectural profession. Philosophies come and go. In the 1960s modernism introduced new techniques and ideas that led to a wave of innovation which was exciting and achieved much, but often with ruthless disregard for context. Public reaction to this led to a loss of confidence and an over-cautious approach in which gimmicks were applied to buildings in a superficial attempt to relate them to their setting. Buildings of this era soon became dated. Gradually architects have rebuilt confidence in an approach which is genuinely modern, but also contextual. Modern materials and construction techniques are utilised in a manner that also considers the special character of the surroundings.

This success could now be compromised as some architects seem to have lost interest in this approach, and now compete to create the most extraordinary forms to make their design more iconic than the last. The result, increasingly, is the creation of gimmicks rather than appropriate responses to brief or surroundings, forms that could be anywhere. The use of computer technology can help the designer make peculiar and amorphous facades that relate to neither internal function nor setting.

Concern for the environment and reducing consumption of energy could restore focus and sense. The external skin of a building is becoming a key generator of the design for entirely logical reasons, helping to moderate between the controlled environment of the interior and external conditions: just as the human skin fulfils a similar function.

This third, vital ingredient forms, with the client's requirements and the response to setting, a trilogy of influences: need, context and environment are the modern equivalent of firmness, commodity and delight (Vitruvius, *De architectura libri decem*, *Ten Books on Architecture*); to these must be added time and cost constraints. As concern for the world's resources and the impact that we are having on our environment increase, so this factor will grow in influence, and the current gluttony of materials being transported across the world will soon be seen as excessive over-indulgence.

With improved transportation we have been able to use a wider and wider range of materials: vernacular architecture receded as the industrial age enabled materials from another region to be moved by canal or train across a country, and now with improved knowledge and communication, ideas and materials are accessible and available across the globe. Contextualism was once an inevitable and unavoidable consequence of limited opportunities; now it is more arbitrary given the lack of boundaries and the powerful technology available to us. But, increasingly now, decisions made for sound sustainable reasons—adapting rather than demolishing existing structures; reusing rather than discarding building materials; avoiding excessive transportation in importing products from afar—all reinforce the argument for a more local contextualism rather than 'international styles'.

Why do we, or should we, value context? First, because it is familiar. This has value to us, as it reinforces a sense of belonging. Secondly, the setting may be of historical importance or interest: its uniqueness is its value. Thirdly, because it has significance, ranging from only local value to national or even international importance.

How should we respond to context? Too often, this is done in a way which is superficial. Use of local materials and matching the scale of nearby buildings does not make good architecture: there are more than enough insipid housing developments that fulfil these narrow aims to make this point. A deeper understanding of context is needed, and from this more informed design decisions made. For example, one of the fundamental purposes of buildings is to create a controlled environment in which activities can take place. This control can be achieved by working with the local climate, or against it. Vernacular forms take into account the prevailing wind, the location of the sun, and use the natural lie of the land to make construction easy and economic. We are now using modern technology and techniques in what is no more than a more sophisticated version of vernacular architecture, using the local micro-climate to reduce energy consumption.

Above all else, contextualism is about harmony, between mankind and the natural and built environment. There is a place for discord, but this only has impact if, in general, there is unity. Buildings which are important and therefore rightly iconic can only stand out and be special if the majority are contextual. It is also important to emphasise that to be contextual does not mean to be the same: to copy what is already there. Far from it: sometimes a contrast is the best way to enhance the ensemble. What is important is that it is done knowingly, a deliberate variation in which the whole composition works together. A fine example of this can be seen from The Backs in Cambridge, where at King's College James Gibbs' Fellows' Building was added alongside the towering verticality of the Gothic Chapel. Another Gothic building

Good contextualism does not mean matching buildings: it can involve contrast in styles, materials and massing. For example, this can be seen in the Cambridge College courtyards, where the domestic scale of Medieval brick ranges contrast with grander stone buildings, containing the college chapels, library and dining halls. At King's College, there is a complementary contrast between the verticality of the Gothic Chapel and the later Fellows' Building, for which James Gibbs chose a Classical style and low horizontal emphasis.

would have added little; instead the low horizontal form and classical styling forms a dramatic counter to its neighbour. It is contextual.

What is neither polite nor contextual is a building with an overblown sense of its own importance: a design that breaks the order without justification. Good architecture arises from an honest appraisal of the significance of the building within its context, and this hierarchy of importance will be represented by how 'loud' or 'quiet' the building is. The Pompidou Centre in Paris by Renzo Piano and Richard Rogers fulfils a major cultural role and is therefore a very significant building, justifying the contrasting materials and forms with its surrounding, and more modest, stone terraced buildings. In spite of the way it breaks the rules, it is contextual because of the way that it creates a public space between it and surrounding buildings; it reinforces pedestrian routes, and organises its circulation to relate dramatically to the public realm.

There is a beautiful consistency of scale, tone and texture to Paris. Neighbouring buildings complement one another through this uniformity. There is still a place for differences, and perversely one can argue that the Pompidou Centre—strikingly different in its materials, colour and assembly—is contextual. It is an important civic building which warrants the differences, but it enhances its neighbourhood, creates new urban places, and respects the scale of street lines and city blocks.

The flaw in this argument is, what about a building with a relatively ordinary function yet which is raised beyond its status by the grandeur of its statement? It could become an important building, much visited, in spite of its ordinary status and it is therefore appropriate for it to stand out and be different from its context for that reason. The answer is, in the hands of a master, this is fine.

In summary and returning to the main theme of this section, our work reflects the widespread concern in the architectural community for producing designs that do respond to their surroundings. The Modern movement produced buildings that ruthlessly explored new ideas that expressed internal function and ignored their surroundings. Opposition to this philosophy was widespread and a period of ultra-conservatism followed; from this has emerged an approach which combines a rigorous and logical expression of the brief, to greater awareness of the need to respond to context.

James Strike, in his book *Architecture in Conservation: Managing Development at Historic Sites*, 1994, discusses these philosophical issues and advocates modern well-designed schemes in historic locations. He points out that HRH the Prince of Wales' book *A Vision of Britain*, 1989, gave a contrary impression, but Strike then quotes an article we wrote at the time to counter this conservative thinking. In particular, we took the Prince of Wales' "Ten Principles" and used a scheme of ours to demonstrate that these aspirations could be met by Modernist solutions just as well.

Re-reading our arguments from then (see caption page 103), one wonders why the debate was even necessary: architecture has moved on so much and gained in confidence by producing high-class schemes that successfully relate to context whilst equally exploiting modern opportunities to the full.

That debate won, the issue for today is whether we are now becoming over-confident, ignoring context and producing so many iconic things that in a decade will seem tedious and dated. The antidote to this threat is sustainability: to produce buildings that advance this cause in an integrated way, that provide inspiration out of necessity.

above
Two prestressed white concrete beams span the length of the pool; one continues to support the ridge of the large garage, whilst the other cantilevers to grasp the basement plantroom flue.

below
Frontage to River Thames

James Strike, in his book, *Architecture in Conservation: Managing Development at Historic Sites,* wrote: *"Building Design* magazine carried out a useful examination of the Prince of Wales' design codes. This report, "Principles in perspective", included an analysis by Roger FitzGerald to see how one of his own modernist projects stood up to the Prince's "Ten Principles". The scheme was a swimming pool extension to a large private house overlooking the Thames in Oxfordshire. FitzGerald's point-by-point comparison shows that the Ten Principles can equally be met by good modern architecture. Hierarchy, for example: The extension continues the internal organisation already established by the house: the main accommodation faces towards the river, whilst the service elements and circulation relate to the driveway.

And Harmony: The river elevation of the existing house was carefully analysed, and the existing elements were repeated or re-interpreted in the extension.

And Decoration: Any decoration was derived from necessity, the concrete circles are where access was required for post-tensioning and bolt connections."

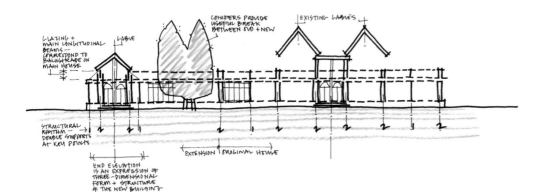

This analysis drawing shows how the new swimming pool extension relates to the context of the adjoining Edwardian House. It does this, in particular, by using its structure and three-dimensional forms to relate to the geometry of the existing building. The whiteness of the river frontage was recognised by the special precast concrete frame of the pool. A pair of post-tensioned beams span longways above the pool; one continues to form the ridge of the garage beyond, whilst the other terminates like a giant fist to support the flue from the basement plantroom.

Analysis

Having got our philosophical approach clear in our minds, how do we then set about developing our understanding of the context? This comes about through careful analysis and avoiding pre-conceived ideas. So, how do we define what the context is? One of the most exciting stages of a project is the keen sense of anticipation as one visits the site for the first time. There is a process of discovery, as you explore the location, stimulating all the senses: the sight of site and views into it and away from it; the sounds—intrusive or not?

With modern compact cameras it is easy to run off plenty of images that capture a record of the appearance of a place. But these are literally snapshots of a moment in time: it is more valuable to dwell for longer, ideally sketching out a place as the process of drawing requires far closer observational skills. Watching people and how they move around or though a site brings a greater understand of its dynamics and potential. What is the public realm—what are the outdoor places around the site, such as streets, public squares, and arcades? How can the scheme enhance these, or help to create them where they are absent?

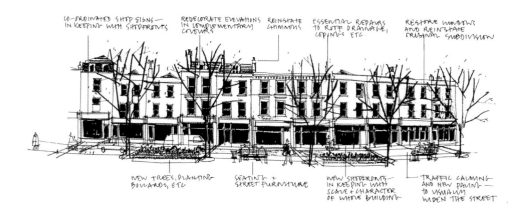

This sketch is a straightforward analysis of part of Rochester as part of a series of proposals to regenerate the town centre; the point is that freehand drawings are often the most effective way of analysing the townscape's character.

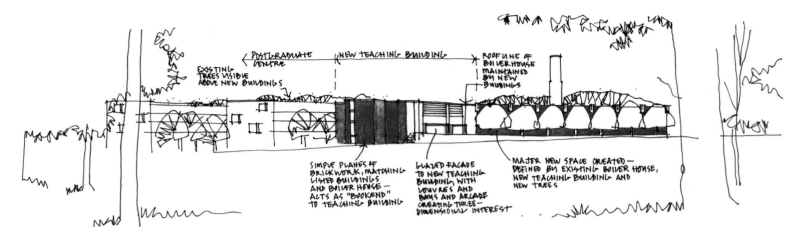

The architectural character of an area should be analysed and understood. This is not to say that new buildings should replicate this character; to the contrary there may be a case for contrast, so long as this is informed, deliberate and for a reason. More fundamental than character, is there an underlying 'grain': a street pattern for example, predominance of organisational devices like courtyards or city squares, or layouts derived from natural features such as the natural fall of the land or the course of a river?

Buildings are experienced and used by people, moving through an area, either by foot or by means of transport. How will they approach the building and enter it; how will it be serviced? A building will not relate successfully to its context unless that context is thoroughly understood, and this can only be achieved by a careful and considered appraisal. Each analysis will be unique, and the level of detail required dependent on particular circumstances. Various devices are used to prepare the study, ranging from aerial photography to freehand sketches; historic maps to local planning policy documents.

We are now going to look at contextualism, from grand scale of regionalism, through urban design and masterplanning, to streetscene, design in sensitive locations and historic buildings.

ADP has prepared a masterplan to develop Sir Basil Spence's campus at the University of Sussex. Spence referred to an aim which was so that users of the campus "could find peace with his visual, oral and nasal senses undisturbed" (Basil Spence, "Building a New University: The First Phase" in David Daiches *The Idea of a New University*, *An Experiment in Sussex*, 1964).

In developing a strategy for the University of Sussex, extending the original campus design by Sir Basil Spence, we wanted to understand the concepts and rationale behind his original vision for the site. This understanding was gained by research particularly of the University's own archive material, and by observation of the site. Spence's design was highly contextual, responding to the opportunities presented by the surrounding landscape, maintaining views between and over buildings to the Downlands beyond, and using a series of interlocking courtyards to generate a flexible layout of attractive external spaces around which to accommodate building functions. Parking and servicing has been kept to the perimeter of the site. The masterplan approach that has emerged is consistent with the principles of Spence's original layout, but also creates opportunities for diversity as well. It is important that a framework is created that exploits the best of the past, so that if divergent buildings or spaces are created this is done knowingly and deliberately, rather than through any lack of understanding of what makes the campus special.

In preparing our designs for a new teaching and residencies development we experimented with similar charcoal drawing techniques used by Spence.

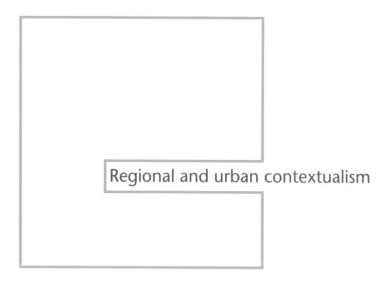

Regional and urban contextualism

Britain has diverse regional characteristics which can provide both design inspiration and restraints. Part of the initial site appraisal should consider the context at this broadest of levels: what is the nature of the landform, the local rock formation, and the natural landscape? How do buildings sit in the landscape, is stone commonly used, and what trees are most prevalent? This is not to say that new buildings and landscaping must follow these precedents, but the designer should be aware of them, and diverge from them deliberately and for a purpose, not by accident or lack of understanding.

However, before discussing the physical context further, the broader consideration is what is the wider impact of a building on a region, in a political, economic and cultural sense? Building projects can have significant effect on a region. For example, although not eventually built in the form envisaged at the time, working with Rummey Design Associates, we prepared plans for an entire new campus for the University of Exeter, in Cornwall. A complete new campus would have acted as a significant economic regeneration tool for a region currently over-dependent on tourism. What was striking was that instead of reacting against such a large-scale scheme (which would have caused uproar in the southeast), local authorities greeted the idea with enthusiasm, keen to see the new campus enhancing their local community. The political and economic benefits of such a large scheme would have been vast. The content of the campus reflected its location, so for example the student accommodation was designed so that it could be used in the summer months as holiday homes.

For the University of Derby we have created a new satellite campus, less than a mile from its main site. Rather than in leafy Allestree, the expansion is closer to the town centre alongside terraced housing. Here, students will work and study alongside the local community, and there should be mutual benefit from the close association. As Higher Education becomes ever more commonplace, remote ivory towers seem less and less appropriate, and close integration of students with local residents, sharing new facilities and mutually supporting local small businesses, highly desirable. These wider aims were, of course, known to the University. The Dean of the Faculty of Arts,

Design and Technology, Professor David Manley, spoke in the early days of the project of how it would transform the City of Derby, celebrating the status of the campus as the first bespoke arts, design and technology campus built in England in the twenty-first century.

There is a balance to be struck here, and this is a theme that runs throughout this book. Regional benefit from architecture cannot only be achieved by gleaming and expensive lottery-funded iconic buildings that close due to lack of demand after a few years of disappointing visitor numbers. Projects such as the University of Derby scheme are based on substance: there is a genuine need in the first place. That need includes a requirement to open within a short time-frame: once funding has been secured there is no reason to delay, and indeed, frequently funds are conditional upon expenditure being incurred within a certain period. Finally, and this is where balance and proportionality is required, the local community will hardly welcome buildings which are clearly over-elaborate and expensive. New buildings in this situation should uplift and inspire, be open and welcoming, but avoid being excessively costly. Tight funding provisions necessitate this anyway, and effective use of limited resources is a skill in itself. The regional benefit arises through integration of the local community, rather than alienation. Buildings should respect and strengthen the local social context, offering opportunity without being patronising.

Overleaf
New university buildings are capable of transforming not only their immediate surroundings, but also contributing to the regeneration of a much wider area. Many of the newer universities were formerly polytechnics or technical colleges; for instance, the University of Derby can be traced back through the Derby College of Art and Technology to its origins in 1851. Its new status, gained in 1992, as a university gave it enhanced standing and its impact at a regional level in providing for the educational and training needs of the local population was increased by the link in 1998 with High Peak College in Buxton. The new satellite campus provides the institution with new buildings of higher quality, clearly distinct from historical associations. This first phase is the Faculty of Arts, Design and Technology.

Below
Further analysis drawings of urban context, Rochester.

Regional and urban contextualism

The architect has a special responsibility when designing in urban situations: here architecture helps shape the everyday behaviour and experience of the public. The street, square, courtyard, alleyway, arcade are all defined by built form, creating places which contribute to the success—or otherwise—of the town or city which the local community occupies.

Good architectural design helps to form these urban settings, giving architects particular responsibility that goes beyond their duty to their clients to a wider social context. Often, a site being redeveloped in an urban setting has potential to add value to its surroundings, acting as a regenerator to an area, attracting investment. The impact of this might be enhanced if the urban site can strengthen its connections to its context, particularly encouraging the creation of new pedestrian routes from the adjoining district through the site.

The unique architectural character of site should be identified, including the spaces between the buildings. New development should take this character into account, reinforcing special and local strengths. There may be a need and an opportunity to 'stitch' a site back together by developing a consistent language that can be applied across the whole of the urban area. Whilst any historic or listed buildings might be conserved in a way that retains their essential qualities that lead to a desire to preserve them, a striking contrast can be created by expressing new elements as a distinctive separate 'layer of history', providing a creative tension and contrast between old and new. This will enable the different periods in history to be legible, with contemporary materials and detailing intervening with the historic fabric. Clear and crisp detailing of contemporary work actually enhances the patina of age.

An unsightly upper floor was removed from the historic lower level and replaced by two new floors, to the C wing at Oxford Castle. The new work is clearly distinct from the original, and even when it weathers over time it will be clearly legible and of a different period to the older base.

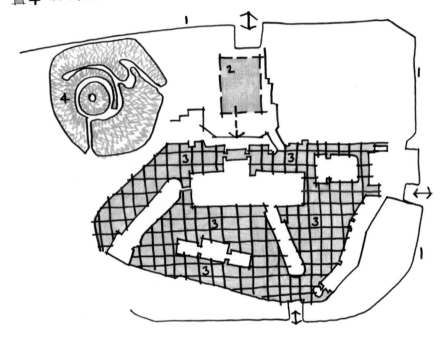

1 STREETSCENE
2 NEW FORMAL SQUARE – ENTRANCE TO HOTEL
3 NEW URBAN SPACES – WITHIN THE WALLS
4 THE MOUND

top
The diversity of the buildings and the spaces between them was one of the great strengths of the Oxford Castle site: we felt from the outset that this complexity could be unlocked by a consistent approach to common themes. For example, where the scheme appears in the surrounding streetscene, the creation of a grand new square on axis with the main entrance to the hotel, the spaces of varied shape and scale between buildings within the walls, and the interface with the Castle mound.

bottom
Extensive consultation took place as part of the scheme to regenerate this site. Wherever possible, it has been open up, to recreate original entrances, to create new buildings where once old ones were, to enhance awareness of the site and allow for new views into and across it.

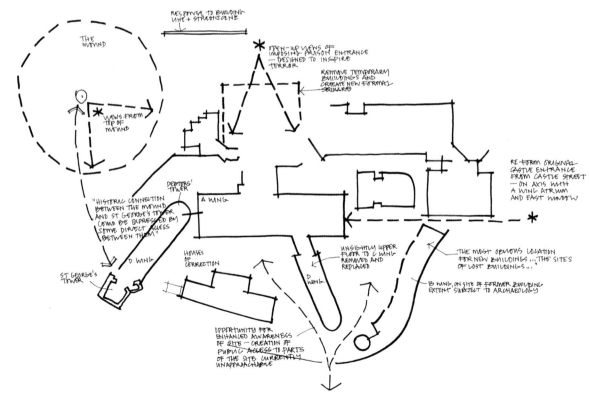

ADP has produced new work in many historic urban settings: in Bath, Cambridge, Canterbury, Oxford, Westminster and Winchester. Of all the projects we have undertaken, the principles outlined above are best demonstrated by a major regeneration of Oxford Castle. 1,000 years of history has had another layer added. All the historically and architecturally significant buildings on the site were retained and carefully restored. They have been converted from their function as a prison to a hotel, a sympathetic use broadly in keeping with their former purpose.

The Castle, closed off whilst in use as a prison, has been restored to the people of Oxford, with vibrant new uses such as restaurants and bars that encourage people in, to use the site. New pedestrian links have been made to surrounding streets, enabling people to pass through the area and linking other urban zones to the city centre.

New external spaces have been created. These are not collegiate quadrangles for which Oxford is famed, but urban, dynamic spaces with seating areas overflowing from the cafes and bars that surround them. As a result, public access and circulation through the site has been improved and people are encouraged to spend time within the scheme, greatly increasing use of the site, integrating the development into the city. An ancient and forgotten quarter of a major city has been given a new historical and cultural purpose; this has been done in a way that works with its intrinsic architectural character.

The design language for this is consistent, from the smallest detail to the overall approach. Where historic buildings or fabric have been kept, this has been preserved. Additions and alterations are distinct, differentiating new from old.

In addition to altering the existing buildings, a major new form has been added, known as B wing. This large new building follows the line of the existing surviving Castle wall with new openings formed through it, one on axis with the end gable of the dominant block, known as A wing. Together with the retained existing buildings, B wing creates a new and dynamic urban space, its shape generated by the geometry of the prison wall. This response to context is also expressed by giant triangular vertical ducts, which act like 'hinges' as the building cranks forwards and back.

C wing had unsympathetic additions to the original fabric (including a complete floor level) and these have been removed to be replaced with two simple, contemporary stone and glass extra floors (see photographs page 111). Throughout the site one comes across small-scale interventions where contemporary glass elements enhance the quality of the original stone building. These interventions arose from a design philosophy which we established early on, including a series of principles. The site is very diverse, and needed to be unified through a consistent language dealing with how the new would be expressed against the old, the character of urban spaces that would be created, and how movement through the scheme would open up the site to link with the surrounding public realm.

Between two surviving wings of the 'Houses of Correction' a new building has been inserted. This occupies the footprint of a previous building but its detailing is clearly modern. The facades incorporate timber panels and large sheets of glass to contrast with the heavy masonry on either side, and to minimise the archaeological impact of foundations by touching the ground as lightly as possible. St George's Tower in background.

In the central atrium a fire strategy was developed that allowed the openness of the space to be retained. To bring balustrades up to current standards, glass has been added whilst retaining the distinctive original metalwork. Redundant cell doors—only around one in three are needed as adjacent cells have been amalgamated to form bedroom suites—have simply been locked shut.

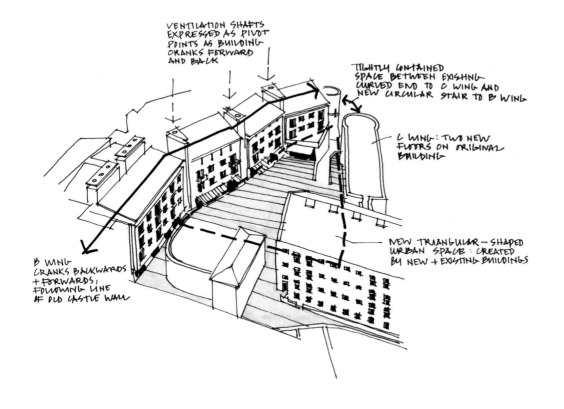

VENTILATION SHAFTS
EXPRESSED AS PIVOT
POINTS AS BUILDING
CRANKS FORWARD
AND BACK

TIGHTLY CONTAINED
SPACE BETWEEN EXISTING
CURVED END TO C WING AND
NEW CIRCULAR STAIR TO B WING

C WING: TWO NEW
FLOORS ON ORIGINAL
BUILDING

NEW TRIANGULAR-SHAPED
URBAN SPACE: CREATED
BY NEW + EXISTING BUILDINGS

B WING
CRANKS BACKWARDS
+ FORWARDS,
FOLLOWING LINE
OF OLD CASTLE WALL

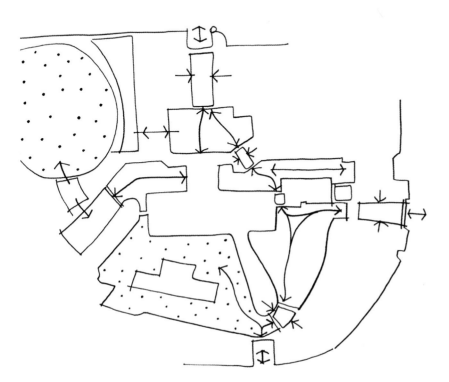

top
A new building, B wing, follows the line of
the Castle wall and creates a new, roughly
triangular urban space with the original
buildings: A wing, C wing, and the Governor's
office. The latter two buildings were both
extended with unsightly additions removed, so
the effect is roughly half original and half new
buildings. At the south end the space narrows,
and a new circular stair tower marks the end of
B wing, mirroring the curved end to C wing.

Oxford is famed for its collegiate quadrangles:
introverted and essentially private spaces with
origins in the monastic cloister and the layout
of the great Medieval manor houses. As part
of the Oxford Castle development, we have
created a very different external space for the
city, urban and public. It is more like the type
of space found in Italy or France, an informal
shape, surrounded by cafes and bars that flow
out into the main area. At the upper levels,
the facade defines the external space, and
balconies provide opportunities for residents to
contribute to the lively character of the space,
bringing vitality to the upper levels as well.

bottom
This is an early design development study,
not of buildings, but of the spaces between
them. The external spaces at the Castle are
immensely varied in shape and scale. In one
respect, this is not dissimilar to the contrasting
spatial sequence experienced in passing
from one collegiate quadrangle to another:
one passes through a gatehouse or similar
restricted space, before reaching a much larger
space. At the Castle, however, the spaces are
less formal and more dynamic: more 'urban'
in character. This is not inappropriate or
surprising as the site is after all 'town' rather
than 'gown'.

Old and new at Oxford Castle. The rugged original stonework of A wing and C wing has been retained; the heavy texture, historic patina and mellow colour of the stonework is offset by crisply detailed and smooth modern glasswork.

An unsightly addition to C wing was removed and replaced by two storeys of new accommodation in a stripped-down minimalist version of the historic stone facades (seen in the photograph, top right). The two wings are linked by a simple glazed connection, whilst the original jail windows have been supplemented by modern windows at a lower height, seen at the extreme left of the image. The modernism of this insertion is emphasised by positioning the windows right at the front of the new opening, flush with the stonework, clearly distinct from the deeply recessed original cell windows. In the new stone facade the windows, being contemporary, are also right forward in relation to their reveals. Old and new are in harmony, but remain distinctly legible layers of history.

The General Design Principles we wrote to guide us in the Oxford Castle project:

- To ensure that design proposals are responsive to functional requirements—just as the historic buildings were designed to meet the needs of their time.

- Equally, designs should respond to the unique and outstanding characteristics and context of the site.

- There should be a consistent 'language' across the whole site to deal with the various degrees of architectural intervention.

- Repairs—and future maintenance—of the historic buildings should be properly carried out in accordance with the appropriate conservation principles.

- The approach to these repairs should be one of the minimum possible intervention, avoiding over-restoration.

- Alterations to the existing buildings should, where possible, be reversible. New work should be distinct from the original, and avoid detracting from it by being clean, simple and unfussy.

- New additions—extensions to existing buildings or new structures—should be of a contemporary style. New work should be simple and allow the existing buildings to be more dominant.

- New work should use materials sympathetic to those already on the site—such as stone, glass, metal and timber—but assembled in a contemporary manner.

- New building techniques and structural solutions should be used where they are developed naturally from the requirements of the brief.

- All design should be of a high quality, appropriate to the outstanding importance and potential of the site.

- All design should be informed by thorough knowledge and analysis of the site and its buildings.

- Design solutions should seek to minimise the damage to areas of archaeological importance.

In summary, the principles outlined above are based on an attitude that sees this current process as just another stage in the long, rich and continuous history of Oxford Castle. We then wrote more detailed assessment and design approaches for the various different parts of the project, within this overall philosophy. Whilst the execution of the approach has changed somewhat due to commercial and other pressures that inevitably arise on a scheme of this complexity, and with the involvement of many other stakeholders, the guiding concepts have been upheld and a diverse scheme successfully unified through contemporary modern insertions that have regenerated a whole forgotten urban area. Now, adjoining sites are being redeveloped, inspired by the Castle development and linking through it to the city centre.

In designing in urban situations, it is vital to respect the 'natural' architectural and historic hierarchy. Some buildings are focal points: the town hall, cathedral, castle, bridge, statues and fountains. For these to be dominant, other elements have to be subservient, providing the calming background that merely reinforces the impact of the main features. Housing, offices, shops and so on provide these parts, and in quantity these predominate. The danger is that clients and architects want their scheme to draw attention to themselves when their status does not warrant this. A 'background' building can still surprise and delight, but within a framework that respects hierarchy.

Of all the historic towns and cities in which ADP has worked, it is in Oxford that we have had the greatest impact, through the sheer volume of work undertaken. Much of this work has involved simple restorations and minor additions, sometimes a complete new building, but individually they represent relatively small changes to the urban fabric. Because we know the city so well, such changes consolidate the essential character of the city. The finest buildings are left unchallenged because the finest are also the most significant; Oxford derives its qualities from its external spaces—the collegiate quadrangles—more than from the buildings that surround and define those spaces.

Oxford is a city with a rich architectural heritage. Elsewhere, and more often, the urban context has less to offer, and new architecture has to fulfil a wider role, helping to shape an improved environment for the future. A good example is in Aston, where our new Business School development was surrounded by uninspiring buildings and disjointed external space. Built alongside one of Sir Basil Spence's less accomplished designs, we have created a new courtyard with the existing buildings, and a new major presence in terms of the surrounding urban area. Lecture theatres were positioned on the ground floor and expressed as curvaceous and eye-catching shapes that exploit their potential to add interest to the composition. The new activity generated by the building and the quality of forms and materials have generated new vitality in the area, and further investment will improve the urban context still further.

The Aston Business School Conference Centre has strong international links, involving curriculum development, recruitment, study visits and events. Our new buildings played an important part in the relaunch of the School, in which strong links with the local business community and industry play a vital part. A new L-shaped building combines with the refurbished original structure to provide new facilities including a 260-seat restaurant, 163 contemporary study bedrooms, cosmopolitan lounge bar and modern new lecture theatres and seminar rooms. Occupying a prominent position in the campus the School fulfils an important role, both in terms of its physical presence but equally in how it operates with local business. There is mutual benefit in the relationship, the School gaining from local knowledge and expertise, and business forging links with a potential source of new talent.

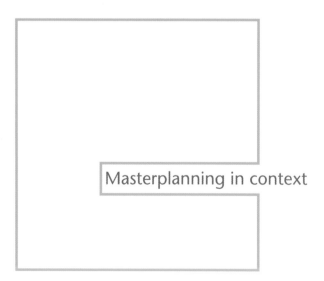

Masterplanning in context

As seen in the first part of this book, much of our work is for large institutions which occupy grand campuses, big enough to create their own micro-context. In many cases these have developed over many years around a core of original purpose-built buildings, which have been extended over a long period to create a unique sense of place. Sometimes this will relate to the local architectural style and materials, sometimes there is a closer relationship to the fashion of the day in which it was built.

All too frequently, a strong original vision for a site, often created by a leading architect of the time, has been compromised by later piecemeal development that does not relate to the earlier work. Strong formal layouts have been compromised by later additions, and new styles of architecture brought in. Often, this has happened in an ad hoc manner, and the task of a new masterplan is first to redefine and reinforce the original sense of place: frequently this is what the institution most cherishes and sometimes these buildings are now listed. The challenge is how to make some sense of the later additions, getting the best use of the existing building stock, and then creating a new plan for future development that creates a strong sense of place, reinforces the history and ethos of the institution, and provides opportunities for growth and vitality in the future.

Great Victorian architecture often forms the centrepiece. Grand layouts were imposed with confidence on the local landscape, and lofty buildings with bold spires and towers created readily identified communities. Chapels, clocktowers, watertowers, dining halls and gateways were given flamboyant expression, gathered around formal quadrangles with immaculate lawns and sweeping drives. Bizarrely, development either side of the Second World War often ignored the obvious opportunity to relate to such a powerful tapestry, and much lower building forms, often of inferior construction with leaky metal windows, flat roofs and mean ceiling heights were constructed, in many cases at peculiar geometries to the original layout.

Christ's Hospital's School's original buildings, with contributions by Hawksmoor and Wren, were in the heart of the City of London. When it was decided to move out, an architectural competition was launched, and won by Aston Webb and Ingress Bell. Their layout took full advantage of the vast site (south of Horsham), ensuring good light and ventilation between the buildings. Chapel, Dining Hall, Library and School Hall were arranged around a Great Quadrangle; set at right angles to this a central avenue had boarding houses on one side and staff houses and gardens on the other. The competition layout was executed largely as the original design, (although the Charities Commission removed some of the excessive architectural features). The site arrangement has served the School well, but a significant change of emphasis has occurred, with vehicular access now no longer approaching along the avenue but instead using an approach on the north-south axis, from the northern side of the site. Together with the addition of new sports facilities, this has changed the focus. Also, teaching accommodation has been added, and further additions will need to retain the confident and formal simplicity of Webb's original layout. The great central space remains the dominant feature, hosting the formal daily march in to lunch, house by house, to the musical accompaniment of the School Band. Our masterplan for the School aims to maximise the potential of the historic buildings without compromising future development.

If only funds would allow for these later additions to be stripped away and to be presented with a blank canvas alongside the original buildings! This is rarely the opportunity: the later additions often have life left in them, and a pragmatic approach is needed, to maximise their usefulness and minimise their impact, drawing together the site in a new vision that creates the context for future designs.

Some institutions are younger, having been founded more recently, or have moved from city centre locations to greenfield sites. The University of Sussex was one of the wave of new universities formed in the 1960s. It appointed Sir Basil Spence to masterplan its site and to design its first buildings. Many of these are now listed, and form the heart of the campus. ADP was commissioned in 2004 by the University to create a new plan to guide development over the next 20 years. We analysed the original concept of Spence's and his vision for the site, this forming the architectural and historical context for new development. We also assessed the impact on the surrounding downland landscape, shortly to form a new National Park. These two influences were complementary: Spence's plan was strongly influenced by the beautiful landscape context, and he wished to retain "enticing glimpses" of the downland between his buildings, and for development to be kept low so that trees would still be visible on the ridgelines beyond.

The campus occupies the valley floor and sides, with fingers of landscape percolating between. Strong formal geometry contrasts with informal belts of trees. We have reinforced the orthogonal Spence layout and, as Spence did, given priority to pedestrians by banishing access roads and parking to the fringes of the site. Great new external spaces will be created, matching the grand focus of Fulton Court. We have been commissioned to design the first part of this plan, which includes 232 new study bedrooms and a new teaching building. These building forms will define new quadrangles and pedestrian routes, and a similar palette of materials—orange/red brick, concrete, copper, flint and glass—will be used, but assembled in a way that reflects the construction techniques of today, rather than those used in the early 1960s.

Spence's approach, which has created a very special university campus, has been strengthened by our plan. We have extended the order, organisation and geometry that Spence began, and integrated form and space within the site, and in how the buildings will sit in the wider land form. But, within this plan we have also identified opportunities for contrasting buildings: special locations for functions that warrant special treatment: an entrance arrival building and social focal points, for example. General teaching, research, administration and residential buildings are viewed as buildings that provide the background setting. This returns us to an earlier theme: the special building will only have added emphasis if there is a general sense of order. If all the new buildings on the campus compete for attention, the result will be lots of gimmicks, a cacophony of forms that diminishes the overall impact.

Analysis of context should focus as much on external space as built form. The University of Sussex derives its special qualities from the landscape and the interlocking courtyards, dominated by Fulton Court, the central space around which Sir Basil Spence's greatest works are gathered. Our masterplan for the future development of the site is organised around similar external spaces, acting as the focal points for outdoor activity and pedestrian movement. The site servicing strategy, car parking and even potential future building forms, are subservient to the external places that will be created. A second great gathering space is planned, not quite of the scale of Fulton Court which will remain the dominant space, but as a grand gesture and organisational device.

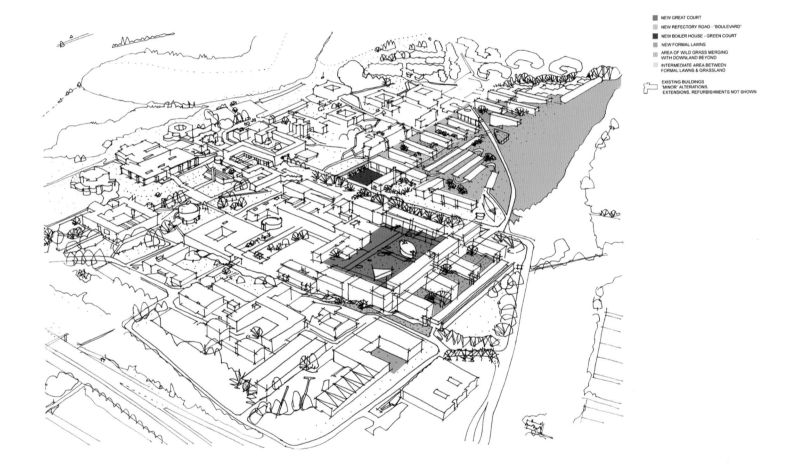

NEW GREAT COURT

NEW REFECTORY ROAD - 'BOULEVARD'

NEW BOILER HOUSE - GREEN COURT

NEW FORMAL LAWNS

AREA OF WILD GRASS MERGING
WITH DOWNLAND BEYOND

INTERMEDIATE AREA BETWEEN
FORMAL LAWNS & GRASSLAND

EXISTING BUILDINGS
'MINOR' ALTERATIONS,
EXTENSIONS, REFURBISHMENTS NOT SHOWN

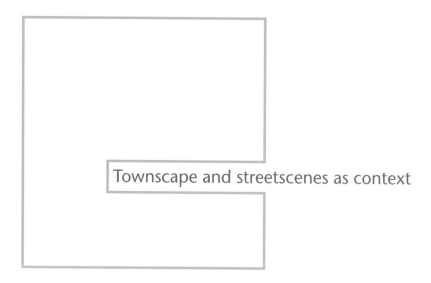

Townscape and streetscenes as context

To what degree should a facade represent the internal arrangement of a building, and to what extent should it respond to its setting? Our approach is to see the elevation as a natural expression of the plan and section, that form evolves from the internal function. Frequently the pressure is to produce a frontage that 'blends' with its neighbours, replicating their height, window pattern and materials. That is fine if they accommodate similar uses, but if not the logic fails, and a facade is imposed on a plan to the detriment of both.

The ultimate folly is represented by schemes where facades are propped up to allow the entire building behind to be demolished and replaced: a complete lack of faith that the profession can produce good quality contemporary additions to the streetscene. Whereas until recently we were producing facades that relate to the interior behind, now there is increasing interest in frontages as a skin, at its best, a thin machine that regulates external conditions to suit the interior it contains.

Streetscenes are at their most vibrant when there is an eclectic mixture of scale, form and style, each period in history adding its own contribution. And yet, the opportunities now are so diverse, this cannot be a licence to produce just anything: our own addition has to have regard for neighbours so that the composition hangs together, that it is better than the sum of all the parts that contribute to its whole. An orchestra makes a more stimulating and diverse sound than the instruments on their own, but it's no good if one person plays jazz if everyone else is playing classical.

Each situation has to be assessed as a unique piece of townscape. Sometimes, there will be the need for a superb piece of restoration work where the architect's contribution will be completely unobtrusive and unknown. On other occasions, a strong contrast is needed: a modern insertion that is the exact opposite of everything else and both benefit from the counterfoil. Elsewhere, a new insertion is just the next one in an eclectic mixture.

As this photograph shows, The Lasdun Building at Christ's College, Cambridge turned its back on the town and the intimate scale of King Street. In 1992 ADP was commissioned to reinstate the streetscene.

In Oxford, we have produced examples of all three. On Cornmarket we have inserted a simple modern glass elevation that contrasts with solid frontages on either side, announcing the shopping mall behind. We have restored an ancient timber structure, taking it apart to repair it and reassemble it: a moment of care and conservation in the building's long history, saving it for future generations. We have added a building that is unique and makes its own contribution. If this seems rather pragmatic, so be it. Appropriateness is more important than a rigid philosophy. Quality of response to context is more important than having a fixed ADP practice style.

In both Oxford and Cambridge, the interplay between 'town' and 'gown' is fraught with tension. Whilst both cities benefit from the academic strength of their universities and gain from the tourism that they attract, interests frequently diverge and lead to jealousy and controversy.

In the long-distant past this has led to social unrest, but an architectural consequence of such divergence can be seen in King Street, in Cambridge. In the 1960s, knowing that there were plans (which were never realised) to widen the road to take more traffic, three Colleges, Sidney Sussex, Jesus and Christ's, employed Howell, Killick,

Partridge and Amis, 1967–1970, Ivor Smith, 1968–1970, and Sir Denys Lasdun, 1968–1970, respectively, to build large new College buildings. These ignored the sinuous alignment and intimate scale of the previously quaint streetscene.

Each of these schemes made no reference to the streetscene and failed to take precedence from the many college buildings in the city which successfully focus inwards towards their collegiate courtyards whilst also responding to the streetscene. Even basic devices such as following the street frontage were ignored, leaving odd-shaped service areas between the college buildings and the streetline. By far the most aggressive was the scheme by Lasdun, which turned its back on the town, placing all study bedrooms on the south side facing in towards the College, with car parking and all ancillary facilities towering over King Street, casting an enormous shadow over it.

All this led to a dramatic headline in *The Architectural Review*: "Anarchy" it screamed, in an editorial which lamented the brash lack of consideration for context: "... it is unforgivable that a great consensus of brains and sensibility were absolutely unable to co-ordinate the new buildings with each other and the existing street". (The Editors, "Anarchy", *The Architectural Review* 1971, no. 895, vol. 150, p. 130.)

Many years later, in 1992, ADP won a limited competition to build a new frontage to Christ's College, between the Lasdun building and the King Street pavement. Sir Denys Lasdun's practice was one of five other firms that we defeated in winning the commission. Our solution mediated between the raw, brutalism of the Lasdun building and the intimacy of the street frontage, repairing the scale and character of King Street.

It achieves this by recognising the rhythm of the historic street, identifying the traditional burgage plot width and modulating the facade to similar widths. Whilst developing this pattern, it also relates to the structural grid of the Lasdun building. The materials, brick and stone, have been articulated in an attempt to respond to the way Lasdun cleverly expressed his precast concrete components, whilst satisfying the college's desire for a more conventional approach.

opposite and below
Our new student accommmodation and retail development for Christ's College in Cambridge mediates between the austere brutalism of this side of the Lasdun Building and the intimate scale of King Street.

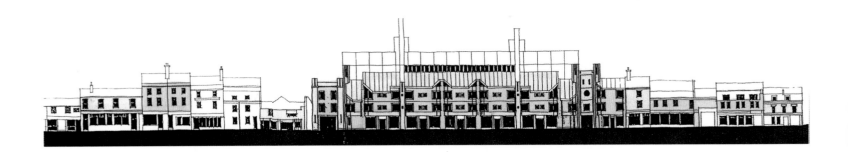

Townscape and streetscenes as context

Adding to historic buildings and conservation areas

Usually, this would be our approach to adding new elements to an historic building, even one of international historic and architectural significance. Sometimes however a different philosophy will be required, particularly if the work is essentially of a repairing nature. At Reading Town Hall we were commissioned to undertake a complete refurbishment of the building, to provide a variety of community uses. Where new elements are clearly distinct from the original, such as the addition of a new lift within the museum, these have been expressed as glass elements. However, at the south end of the building we replaced bomb damaged areas with a new clocktower, and here it was more appropriate to do so in the style of the original architect, Sir Alfred Waterhouse.

Following relocation of the Borough Council's administrative functions to new Civic Offices, ADP won an architectural competition to bring the whole of the original Town Hall into community use. This included restoration of the Small Town Hall of 1785 and Sir Alfred Waterhouse's Victorian building, dating from 1875. The latter suffered bomb damage in the Second World War, and ADP designed a new clocktower in keeping with Waterhouse's work (right tower, photo on left). This was a forerunner of a more relaxed approach to the conservation of listed buildings, in which both modern insertions totally distinct from the original and historic repair work can co-exist. The external fabric responds to the context of the exterior of the original envelope, whilst modern insertions have been created within the building (photo, right). By providing fine new facilities, including a museum, concert hall, cinema, cafe, meeting rooms, art gallery and tourist information, the building has become more open and accessible to the local community. New horizontal routes through the building ensure that access is now being provided for all.

Adding to historic buildings and conservation areas

It is perfectly possible to produce contemporary design within conservation areas; indeed, it can be argued that the impact on this context is less if one utilises modern materials that emphasise the qualities of the older structures that contribute to the character of the area.

Likewise, modern methods can diminish the impact of new development within Metropolitan Open Space. Two examples of this strategy can been seen in new work for Highgate School. School House was a former Head Master's House with attached dormitory accommodation, and we combined a careful restoration of this external fabric with a modern internal conversion and extensions to provide a new centre for art and design technology. Adjoining landscape was brought right over the new extensions providing areas of lawn to improve the setting of the Victorian building, whilst housing new technology laboratories concealed below (see page 40).

In the Highgate Village Conservation Area we added a new rooftop extension, subordinating it to the structure below by recessing glass frontages behind the parapets. A bold roof form expressed a structure which takes the loads into the centre of the building, further lightening the appearance of the new elevations, and using modern construction techniques to help assimilate the extension into its context.

Often the settings are tight and urban, but occasionally a conservation area's character is derived from individual villas or pavilions set in gardens. An example is North Oxford, and here we have designed various buildings and extensions. In the grounds of St Antony's College we integrated the Institute of Japanese Studies, a design that was influenced by Japanese architecture and which adds to the diversity of styles within the area (see overleaf).

This scheme for Highgate School adds a new penthouse level to an existing building, using components partly assembled off-site, and providing light and airy new facilities for the School, utilising stunning rooftop views across the City of London. The approach allows the original building to continue to make the significant contribution to the local conservation area, with the light and recessive rooftop addition replacing unsightly later additions and clutter that had accumulated over several years. Although additional accommodation has been created, the streetscene has been enhanced. Two structural solutions were adopted to suit the differing construction of the two wings (see diagrams opposite).

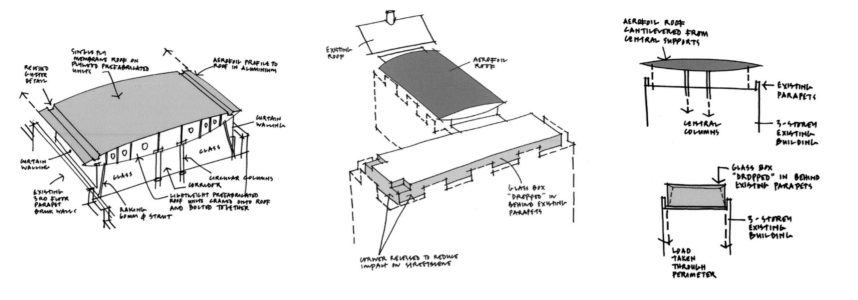

SINGLE PLY MEMBRANE ROOF ON PLYWOOD PREFABRICATED UNITS

REVISED GUTTER DETAIL

AEROFOIL PROFILE TO ROOF IN ALUMINIUM

CURTAIN WALLING

GLASS

CURTAIN WALLING

CIRCULAR COLUMNS

CORRIDOR

EXISTING 3RD FLOOR PARAPET BRICK WALLS

RAKING 60mm ∅ STRUT

LIGHTWEIGHT PREFABRICATED ROOF UNITS CRANED ONTO ROOF AND BOLTED TOGETHER

EXISTING ROOF

AEROFOIL ROOF

GLASS BOX "DROPPED" IN BEHIND EXISTING PARAPETS

CORNER RECESSED TO REDUCE IMPACT ON STREETSCENE

AEROFOIL ROOF CANTILEVERED FROM CENTRAL SUPPORTS

EXISTING PARAPETS

CENTRAL COLUMNS

3-STOREY EXISTING BUILDING

GLASS BOX "DROPPED" IN BEHIND EXISTING PARAPETS

3-STOREY EXISTING BUILDING

LOAD TAKEN THROUGH PERIMETER

Adding to historic buildings and conservation areas

North Oxford has an eclectic mix of architectural styles. The Institute of Japanese Studies provides another unique addition to its Conservation Area setting. Pavilion-like in character, its proportions and simplicity provide an elegant addition to its leafy surroundings. In addition to a new 150-seat lecture theatre, teaching spaces and residential accommodation, the building houses the Bodleian Japanese Library, part of the University's central Bodleian Library.

Adding to historic buildings and conservation areas

Landscape as context

Through history buildings have related to the land form and landscape in which they sit. In the Yorkshire Dales, houses, barns and walls dividing fields are built of the local stone, and appear to almost grow out of the landscape. Fields within the walls are treated with fertiliser and seem greener than rougher grassland beyond, linking the appearance of the grassland to the stone walls that define them. The use of the buildings and their functional design emerge directly from the agriculture that they serve. Landscape and architecture are totally integrated.

Classical country houses present a different approach: stylistic ideas gathered from the Grand Tour or pattern books were imposed, and materials brought from outside the region. Even the surrounding landscape was re-formed to suit the idyll. Architecture is imposed on the setting.

Is the empathy displayed by Sir Alec Clifton Taylor in *The Pattern of English Building*, 1962, to be discarded as a sentimental relic from a bygone age? He demonstrates knowledge and a real feel for the British landscape: its geology and materials and the relationship between the two, and was acutely aware of the need to avoid sentimentalism.

Building uses today rarely relate directly to their surrounding landscape, and materials can now be brought from afar. A desire to relate architecture to a landscape context arises for other reasons, such as a desire to sit a form pleasingly in an attractive setting, or to allow internal uses to flow seamlessly out into the landscape. Frankly, this takes some skill, and as we consume more and more green land, it is vital that this is done in a way that enhances the green space that we leave undeveloped.

Roffey Park Institute occupies a site within an Area of Outstanding Natural Beauty and is within the Strategic Gap between Horsham and Crawley. It maximises its setting as an asset, providing training and seminar facilities in a situation where delegates can relax and enjoy time breaking out from formal training sessions in relaxing surroundings. To meet its requirements for new and improved seminar rooms, dining facilities,

In the Yorkshire Dales, building functions emerge directly from the use of the land, and so do the building forms and materials. Architecture and context are completely integrated. Barns are used by cattle and sheep for shelter, with the upper level for storing hay. Stone walls divide fields and barns are formed from local stone. Where walled enclosures end, some way up the side of valleys, so the greener fertilised pastures give way to the truly natural landscape.

The ultimate expression of architecture and setting at one with each other would be where buildings and walls are built out of the natural local stone: as though growing out of the rock, or hewn from it. Picturesque forms and sagging roofs and drystone walls that follow the lie of the land, as seen in the Yorkshire Dales or the Cotswolds, for example—a romantic contextualism. Classical buildings contrast with this, imposing an order and formality upon the landscape, and if the latter needed shaping a little to enhance the effect, then as demonstrated by Capability Brown (for example, at Chatsworth), the context could be adjusted to create the desired result.

study bedrooms, entrance reception and car parking, we considered carefully how to relate the building to its context. We created two new courtyards, spaces which allow the surrounding landscape to flow between the built forms. Facing into these 'controlled' spaces the facades were designed to be smooth, white and crisp, whilst the outer 'shell' looking out, to the more 'natural' landscape, was tougher and harder. White render on the inside and a rough brick on the outside; we drew an analogy from nature with the smooth inside of a chestnut shell contrasting with the rough surface of the outside. Themes from nature were brought through the development, with curvaceous lime green natural forms of 'thinking pods', and indigenous bluebells planted in the quadrangles also symbolised internally with matching colours in the carpets. Delegates can move easily from inside to outside, and landscape and building create a new and unified context for Roffey at work. The new facility is called "the Meadow" demonstrating how the architectural thinking and client vision were aligned in maximising the asset of the setting.

Whilst Roffey occupies essentially a landscaped environment, our new project for the University of Derby is on a brownfield site at the cusp between urban form and landscape. On one side there is an area of densely packed Victorian terraced housing in a distinctive and rather severe red brick; on the other a stream and natural landscape. The building we have designed emphasises this transition. A central 'street' extends the local Pybus Street on the same axis right through the building, confronting any issues or dilemmas, in terms of relations with the local community, head-on whilst visually linking urban density to open landscape. The accommodation has been arranged into long fingers which allow the landscape to flow into the site and bring natural light and ventilation flooding into the functioning spaces. The stream has been extended with reed beds on the natural landscape side of the building, and large lecture theatres, expressed as free forms, reflect the natural aspects of the site.

Contextualism

The new conference and training facilities at Roffey Park are advertised as "The Meadow"—space to meet, think and develop. Set within 40 acres of countryside in the midst of St Leonard's Forest, an Area of Outstanding Natural Beauty, there is a symbiosis between landscape and building use. Roffey's particular way of functioning was closely studied and analysed before detailed design proposals were made, and the characteristic style of formal gathering followed by informal break-out sessions are reflected in the rectilinear form of the large seminar room, with curvaceous thinking bubbles or syndicate rooms alongside. The latter are natural shapes, like an egg or an acorn, coloured to match the fresh spring-like colours of the bluebells and birch leaves, both of which feature prominently in the Forest. Whilst these elements relate to the landscape, the dining area occupies "The Orangery" which is situated on the location of a former glasshouse within the original kitchen garden of a large country house. The remnants of the old garden wall remain, giving a historical context to the layout and style of this part of the development.

Overleaf
At Roffey Park Institute a significant new building has been integrated into an Area of Outstanding Natural Beauty. Study bedrooms face into a new courtyard, with white rendered elevations providing a sharp backdrop to silver birch trees, whilst the large seminar facilities have a living room: sedum providing a natural habitat for plants and wildlife.

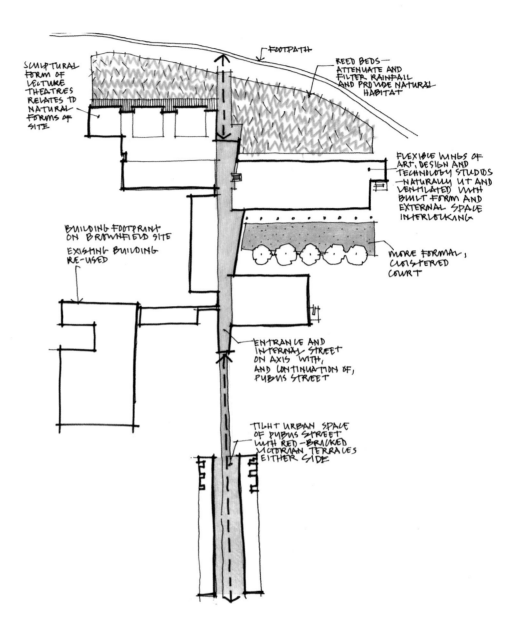

SCULPTURAL FORM OF LECTURE THEATRES RELATES TO NATURAL FORMS OF SITE

FOOTPATH

REED BEDS ATTENUATE AND FILTER RAINFALL AND PROVIDE NATURAL HABITAT

FLEXIBLE WINGS OF ART, DESIGN AND TECHNOLOGY STUDIOS - NATURALLY LIT AND VENTILATED WITH BUILT FORM AND EXTERNAL SPACE INTERLOCKING

BUILDING FOOTPRINT ON BROWNFIELD SITE

EXISTING BUILDING RE-USED

MORE FORMAL, CLOISTERED COURT

ENTRANCE AND INTERNAL STREET ON AXIS WITH, AND CONTINUATION OF, PYBUS STREET

TIGHT URBAN SPACE OF PYBUS STREET WITH RED-BRICKED VICTORIAN TERRACES EITHER SIDE

At the University of Derby our new building mediates between the tight urban scale of Pybus Street and open, informal landscape. The sketch above shows how the Victorian streetline continues right through the new building, whilst fingers of built form project out into the landscape. Building and open space are totally integrated, and the character of the spaces vary, from urban and formal close to the townscape, and open informal reed beds closest to the natural landscape.

141

Landscape as context

The University of Bath occupies a fine site, and adjoins National Trust land. We were commissioned by the University to design new student accommodation at the edge of its site, next to open countryside. We responded to this context by creating an E-shaped layout, with three parallel fingers extending towards the landscape and the main density of study bedrooms therefore as far as possible from it. Just as at Derby, the landscape will alternate with the building fingers, and a graduation of spaces are envisaged, moving from a tightly defined formal space (next to the building reception) to a larger and less formal space, and finally to the biggest and most loosely contained area, (next to the even wider landscape beyond). This sequence of external spaces works hand-in-hand with the internal organisation of study bedrooms. The layout of these addresses issues such as creating appropriate social groupings and suitable provision of access and facilities for all. There is more: the scheme has been designed to achieve a new benchmark "Excellent" level of BREEAM rating for student accommodation. The design therefore brings together three main themes: relationship with landscape setting, internal functional requirements and an environmentally responsible approach. Put another way, context, need and environment—the guiding philosophy outlined in the introductory comments to this section.

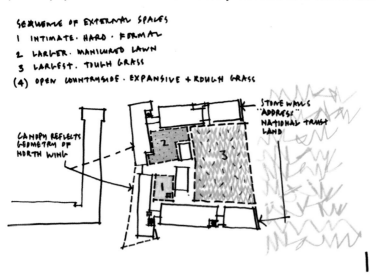

For this new student residence scheme for the University of Bath, the distribution of accommodation on the site reflects what surrounds it: the building forms are arranged around a three-sided courtyard; the fourth open side faces open landscape, with the main focus of activity at the opposite end, closest to the main campus. The arrangement minimises the impact of the project on the adjoining landscape and allows natural light and air into the scheme. The external spaces then become progressively tighter and more urban in their character, so making a transition from the hard landscape of the University campus to the open fields beyond (see early exploratory sketch, left).

Assessment of the context can take place at the first inception of a project, and can influence our approach at the outset. In early 2000 ADP was invited with five other firms to compete for the design of a new infants' school in Riverhead, Sevenoaks. Part of the brief was that it was expected that the proposal would respect its context, and therefore be of brick and tile construction to match the surrounding architectural character. We questioned this, pointing out that the surroundings to the brownfield site were actually greenbelt land and the surviving parkland setting of a former large estate, Montreal Park. Also, steeply pitched tiled roofs create unused roof spaces and imply a narrow planned building whereas we envisaged a deep plan building, giving greater efficiency in use of space (with less circulation) and flexibility to subdivide the space in different ways in the future as teaching methods change.

We won the competition with a design that sweeps the surrounding landscape up to and over the building, a sedum roof integrating architecture and parkland. The north side of the building, facing the busy A25, deals with vehicular and pedestrian access, and internally this side of the building contains the administration and staff areas, kitchen servery and plantroom, and the hall, which can be accessed independently and used out of hours by the local community. The nine classrooms face south, gaining the best views, natural light and ventilation, are shielded from the north winds and traffic, and are given security by the buffer adult zone. One major concern of local residents was the impact of traffic movement and this has been mitigated by a travel plan which has been successfully implemented, including "walking buses"—children walking under adult supervision on designated routes with pick-up points.

Whilst the green roof and sustainable approach are sensitive responses to the context, the design is bold and striking in other respects, making a confident statement of the function of the building. Strong geometric forms 'pop' through the roof, housing the extra height needed for the main hall (a blue cubic form) and the main entrance (triangular and red, representing the school's colours). The School is an important community building—warranting a degree of assertiveness—sitting in a parkland landscape, and our design responds to these contextual influences. Internally it also reinforces the educational objectives of an outstanding school, and thankfully the governors and headteacher had the confidence to select a design both bold and contextual.

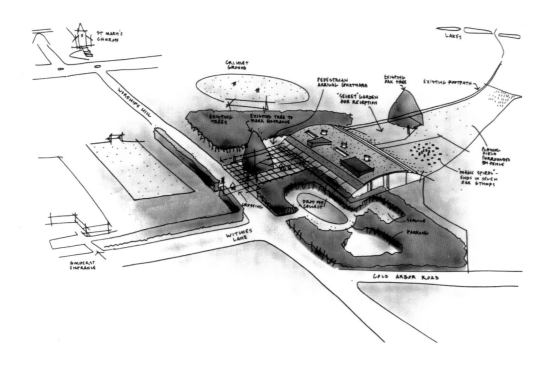

Early concept sketch and its realisation were closely matched at the Riverhead Infants' School, with the landscaped parkland context brought over the roof of the new school. This is a sedum roof, chosen for its lightness, minimising the load on structure, and its low maintenance, requiring no cutting or watering. Its colour changes with the seasons, on occasions presenting a vivid brown/red and at other times a more complementary green.

A commission to design a group of polo stables with supporting accommodation, next to a listed barn and in an Area of Outstanding Natural Beauty, required a different approach. Located close to the River Thames and providing accommodation for one of the top polo teams in the country, we were asked to provide 49 stables, tack rooms, a conference room, support facilities and mini-flats for the polo manager and players.

The site was previously occupied by a group of farm buildings. We carried out studies of the history of built form on the site, local farm groupings and layouts, how buildings sit in the landscape, and the materials and detailing of local buildings. From a distance, the polo complex appears to be a traditional and informal group of buildings. Come closer, and it then becomes clear that the traditional forms and materials have actually been detailed in a contemporary way that reflects the unusual and intriguing commission: a design that reflects the needs of a community of ponies, creating lofty and robust spaces where they can see one another but remain safely confined.

Apart from a farmhouse (far left) and a listed barn (not visible), these are all new buildings integrated into the setting of an Area of Outstanding Natural Beauty on the banks of the River Thames.

In nature, patterns repeat. Where there are repetitive requirements, architecture benefits from a straightforward representation of this. At the Polo Stables complex in Oxfordshire, a series of repeating stables receive the simplest expression, with natural ventilation chimneys breaking the skyline and casting shadows.

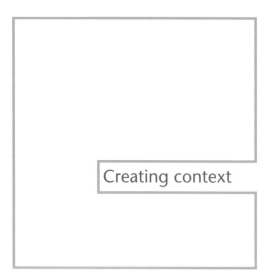

Creating context

Sometimes, a location has little context and it is therefore necessary to create a sense of place to give it some structure and purpose. An example of this is the Oxford Science Park where, working with Rummey Design Associates, ADP has completed several new buildings which, with new landscaping, create a context to help to shape further development. Too often, business parks are anonymous, with developers only concerned with their short-term potential. In only ten years the new landscape, paving, bridges and parking areas (some of which is decked) have become as important as the buildings in creating the character of a delightful place to work.

In many ways these are harder projects to design, where there is little or no context to respond to and a building which needs to simply create flexible space for a user not yet defined: in this situation one has to get to the very core of what the project is about. In the case of the buildings we have provided on the Oxford Science Park, it is to do with how they create new spaces between each other, how they interface with the landscape being formed, and how to provide high quality spaces in which work. Given that the alternative might be to work in the historic and attractive city centre of Oxford, the new environment must compete and surpass this and provide other attractions such as ease of access, tranquil surroundings and modern working environments.

At the Oxford Science Park we have designed small starter business units, office and research space, a restaurant, conference rooms, crèche, bridge links, and car parking areas, all to create an attractive place to work. What succeeds most of all is how these elements are brought together to create a new sense of place, with strong new hard and soft landscaping unifying the building elements. All of this has been created in little more than a decade; what it lacks in history is compensated for by easy-to-use and rapidly maturing external places.

To create a new sense of place at the Oxford Science Park we have created several new buildings, of slightly different approaches, but with consistent attention to detail, careful choice of material, and close integration with the landscape. New, heavily planted courtyards have been formed, car decks created, and riverside walkways delineated. A new bridge provides a dramatic connection across an existing watercourse, joining a refurbished cafe to a new 'incubation' unit—where fledgling businesses can rent flexible space as their ideas develop and organisations start to grow. Next door, we have designed a new nursery, which provides additional diversity to the mixed accommodation of a science park.

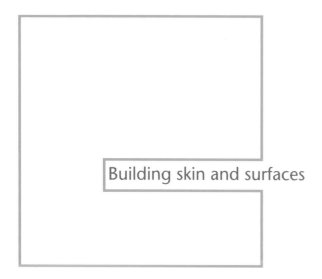

Building skin and surfaces

There is a developing interest in how buildings are wrapped in their surrounding envelope, or skin, treating this as a surface not necessarily derived from the building interior. The external elevations of a building are where the building interior meets the surrounding setting. What has been 'supposed' to happen is that the elevation should be an expression of the internal plan, itself derived from the functional requirement of the building. Equally, this elevation should relate to the context, integrating new building with surroundings. As Robert Venturi puts it in *Complexity and Contradiction in Architecture*:

"Designing from the outside in, as well as the inside out, creates necessary tensions, which help make architecture. Since the inside is different from the outside, the wall— the point of change—becomes an architectural event."

This is now being challenged. The skin can be used to moderate climate. It might incorporate decoration, maybe derived from context, maybe not. The skin dictates the interior, determining how the building functions, and where activities are best placed. Patterns can be brought into the facade treatment, derived from studies of surrounding buildings or topography, local trade, culture or industry. When the interior of a building is required to be as flexible as possible, bringing something ofthe context into the external envelope can be the only way to enliven   what is otherwise an undecorated shed.

There is nothing new in this. Wren's facade at St Paul's creates the right impression of what a classical cathedral frontage should be, but does not actually reflect the scale or form of the nave behind. It is in effect an enormous blank frontispiece with nothing behind it at the upper level. Sir John Soane, in his house at 13 Lincoln's Inn Fields, applied a frontispiece in stonework in front of the original brick elevation: simply one 'skin' of material in front of another.

Recent interest in expressing building envelopes as a series of 'layers' in which different materials are represented distinct from each other is not an entirely new concept. Sir John Soane—innovative and modern in so much of his thinking—introduced this idea to the front facade of his house at 13 Lincoln's Inn Fields, now the Sir John Soane Museum. Built in 1812 and first left as an open loggia, the stone facade created a separate distinct 'layer' to the brick frontage behind.

Our design for a new Learning Centre with student support services for Canterbury Christ Church University requires the creation of large flexible areas. The perfect functional and flexible expression of this would be an enormous shed. This would be daunting in scale for the staff and students using the building, and would be completely unrelated to the city in which it is found. We have therefore articulated the skin of the building, and incised two deep cuts into the building form, relating to two diagonal views out of the building, one to the Cathedral tower and the other to Dane John Mound, an historic burial mound. The front skin of the building will be glazed, a pure and clean membrane, to give a reflection of the city walls opposite. This will give two different interpretations of surface: one as a membrane like the surface tension of a liquid. The other version will be a way of making the facade three-dimensional, by pulling elements out of it and by cutting elements into it.

This current interest in surfaces and skins is a fascinating development. However, too often, we are seeing designs which latch onto this as a new trend, and the same geometric patterns are appearing on projects all over the country. This is unthinking! The patterns should be derived from context, or celebrate the way the facade is made, or provide for the best sustainable envelope for the built form. Any of these, so long as there is an intellectual progression, but not just a copy of an architectural fashion.

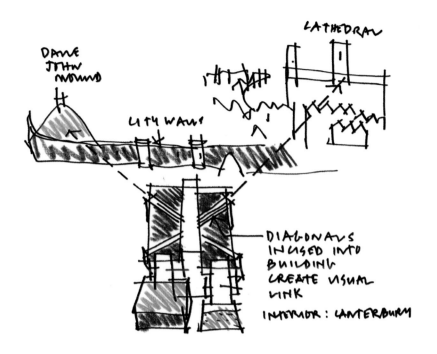

CATHEDRAL

DANE
JOHN
MOUND

CITY WALLS

DIAGONALS
INCISED INTO
BUILDING
CREATE VISUAL
LINK

INTERIOR: CANTERBURY

Just outside the City Walls, but fronting onto the conservation area, our new building for Canterbury Christ Church University establishes visual and symbolic connections to the Cathedral and city walls—diagonal axes that are incised into the built form. These angular connections are also found within the building, with diagonal bridges connecting the two wings on either side of a central atrium.

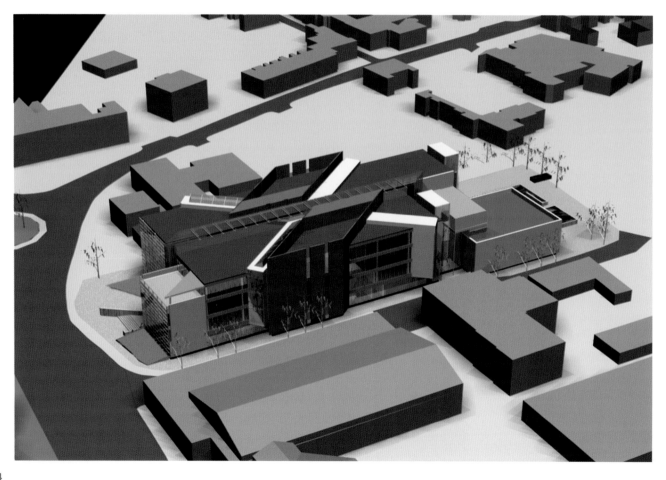

154
Contextualism

We aspire to produce buildings with strong ideas, well executed. By this, we mean that the way that the building is constructed, down to the finest detail, should reinforce the overall design concept. Good design is a continuum, from the broad concept diagram to the way that the building is actually constructed and how that construction, the bringing together of various materials, is handled. Detailing has to consider ever more complex issues. To add to the fundamentals of keeping the weather out, providing a method of fixing, dealing with differential movement, moisture and condensation, new regulations governing thermal performance and acoustics make it harder to express the main components that make up the building. Cover flashings and mastic can easily take over, covering principal elements of structure and losing clarity of junctions between main elements of building fabric.

Reflecting the vital importance of meeting time and cost constraints, other methods of procurement need to be carefully refined to ensure that we maintain control of the detail of how a building is assembled, and in the rush to complete the project, workmanship—particularly of the critical and highly visible finishing trades—can easily suffer.

In designing details it is easy to overlook the issue of building tolerances. Drawings are only a method of communication, whether conveying an idea to a selection panel representing a potential new client, presenting a detailed scheme design to a planning committee, or directing the contractor on what is to be built. Components are manufactured by processes which have inherently variable tolerances depending on human accuracy, shrinkage, movement and so on. Once on site, they are assembled in ways which again depend on those placing and fixing them, frequently in poor weather conditions with surrounding distractions and limited by other factors. This is not to condone poor quality, to the contrary. Architecture is a unique creative act, constrained by others and by time. Architects are detached from the actual process of making the work, indicating through drawings our intentions for execution by others.

The tools at the disposal of the architect have improved, with technical information just a couple of clicks of the mouse away from every workstation, and computers capable of drawing unimaginably complicated three-dimensional geometries. This all helps, but sometimes an old fashioned pencil and scrap of paper remain the quickest way of thoroughly working through a complex detail in all its aspects.

The ability of computers to generate and resolve the most complex shapes and forms has led to some exciting and iconic buildings, which returns us to a point made earlier. It remains to be seen how many of these amorphous blob-shaped and angular buildings our environment can accommodate. Buildings are seen, experienced and used by humans, and whilst complex shapes might be appropriate for a few 'special' or 'iconic' buildings, for less significant functions in the overall hierarchy, a simple 'background' building will suffice. These serve to reinforce and emphasise the more prominent buildings, and a more rational straightforward shape is more likely to be timeless both in terms of style and usefulness.

Because our work is for varied clients with different uses and responds to its individual context, every building is bespoke. Whilst we aim to achieve consistency in our detailing and to learn from past projects refining our approach, there is, as a result, great variety in how our buildings have been assembled. Changing regulations also mean that every detail needs to be thought through in relation to the unique circumstances it has to serve.

Regional character is often provided by the way that builders in the past have passed knowledge from generation to generation, evolving building forms that exploit the natural environment to provide controlled interiors, and using building materials in particular ways. There is no point in replicating these methods for the sake of imitation, but there is the opportunity to abstract and develop historic techniques that exploit natural resources or provide a human and distinctive touch.

Restoration work requires judgement and experience. Too easily, one can be led down the route of over-restoration, having a greater impact than is necessary or desirable. This can apply particularly in the case of commercial developments where the developer client wants a neat and tidy appearance to attract tenants and is not concerned by what is appropriate in conservation terms. At the Market Hall in Winchester, stone and other fabric repairs were taken as far as they need to be, and no further, retaining the natural historic appearance of the building which contributes much to its charm. The developer's needs were fully met and the project successfully transformed a derelict building categorised as being "at risk" into a new use. In this project we distinguished between careful repair of original fabric and the addition of new contemporary elements that reflect the new purpose of the building, adhering to the current philosophy which generally accepts this approach: distinguishing later additions as a new 'layer of history'.

This philosophy applies just as much to alterations and additions to modernist buildings, and increasingly we are being commissioned to revitalise 1960s architecture to meet current needs.

This beautiful doorway simply required some straightforward conservation repair work to integrate it into our development of the Market House, Winchester.

This project represents the most recent phase of refurbishment work undertaken for Brunel University and is an excellent example of 'Mending Modernism'.

The Central Lecture Building is situated in the heart of the campus, a key shared resource used by all students. The original building was designed in the early 1960s to provide the campus with lecture theatres, classrooms, and a media centre. The brutal concrete architecture of the building, with its cantilevered concrete lecture theatres, was used as a backdrop to the film version of *A Clockwork Orange*.

The client's brief was to refurbish and develop this centralised teaching facility and bring all its lecture theatres and classrooms up to modern standards: introducing IT-enriched rooms, flexible teaching arrangements in classrooms, better environmental controls, and a more positive and exciting teaching and learning environment alongside social spaces. This redevelopment is the focal point of the new Uxbridge campus masterplan and considerable consultation was involved in the design development process to ensure new facilities responded to the needs of all subjects.

Our additions exploit the strong backdrop provided by the existing building, whilst providing new, legible and distinctive additions.

Looking to the future: sustainability

In the last chapter we outlined how we set out to design in context, and that we begin this process by careful analysis. We then demonstrated how this has been applied, by reference to a range of scales, from small additions to listed buildings to regional regeneration. Broader still, we touched on wider environmental issues that affect the entire planet. In the opening section on the history of the practice we mentioned that ADP has demonstrated its concern for these questions since the 1980s, and looking to the future we see this taking on ever-increasing significance. As mentioned in the discussion on contextualism, this trend supports our approach, with locally sourced materials and careful response to the local climate and topography more likely to be environmentally responsible than imposing international styles or pre-conceived ideas that take no account of context.

We produce buildings to control our environment: to keep us dry when it rains, cool when it is hot, warm when it is cold. Maintaining this internal environment has far reaching environmental consequences and in the last two decades our understanding of the concept of sustainability and sustainable solutions to such age-old problems has changed significantly. From an elusive and often abused concept, used to justify design solutions ranging from the profoundly considered to mere ornament and gesture, sustainability has become crucial: an intrinsic part of any design, that should be rigorously assessed and applied.

Government funding linked to requirements to consider the environmental impact of projects and the very nature of education clients in particular, encourages socially responsible design. Aside from any kudos attached to sustainable design (government or otherwise), structured analysis of the environmental impacts of a project leads to a better building for the client, building users and society as a whole.

Straightforward examples such as good ventilation, natural daylighting, thermal mass, material choice, orientation or fitting the building to the land form, all lead to buildings that are simply more pleasant to use as well as being more environmentally responsible. Sustainability leads to consideration of life-cycle costs: a prompt to make design decisions at the outset and to test design choices to provide benefits that accrue both financially and in pleasure in use over the many decades of a buildings' life. Thankfully consideration of life-cycle cost is becoming established as best practice.

Sustainable design is a process: a learning cycle with structured analysis at every design stage, from receipt of brief to post-occupancy evaluation—all feeding back into improved knowledge for the next project. This process can be applied to any project: our view is that sustainability is not a style, rather a set of filters to apply to the design process to test and help evolve better buildings. The illustrations in this section demonstrate how consideration of sustainability principles has been a major design generator. In each case, the most important thing is to work with our clients to understand their aims and objectives and to suggest approaches to individual projects which best meet this.

The sustainability 'agenda' should not be imposed, rather discussed and incorporated as best meets the needs of each client—their aims, objectives and philosophy, and without detriment to the core functionality of the building. Our role as architects is to be at the forefront of thinking on approaches to achieving sustainable architecture, to understand technologies and to participate in continuing debate on environmental issues in order to provide well researched and knowledgeable advice to our clients.

From the client's perspective, sustainability is a positive. From early reports such as *Environmental Responsibility: an Agenda for Further and Higher Education* (1992, Chaired by Professor Peter Toyne, Vice-Chancellor, Liverpool John Moore's University), education has been a leading sector for promoting sustainability, not just through qualifications and teaching, but as a means to attract and motivate staff and students, enhance reputations, save money, educate future generations and build relationships with the wider community.

This design for a new school in Devon uses a curvaceous shape and green roof to assimilate the new form into its setting. Natural light and ventilation, ground sourced heating and cooling, rain water harvesting and grey water recycling were integral to the earliest design concepts.

The design continues themes from our Riverhead School design, which has been showcased by the Building Research Establishment as an exemplary sustainable design (see bibliography).

Issues such as carbon neutrality and biodiversity are now being explored by organisations such as The Carbon Trust, The Environmental Association for Universities and Colleges, Eco Schools, and through a key element of the government's own agenda for change in education: Building Schools for the Future.

Architects can help schools, colleges and universities build better, more efficient buildings that improve the environment both within and between the buildings themselves; make better use of available resources and apply appropriate energy saving techniques and materials for environmental gain. We will discuss some key issues, with relevance to ADP projects; an in-depth discussion of these techniques is beyond the scope of this book but such information is widely available elsewhere.

The path to sustainability is not just marked by efficient buildings; the purpose of the buildings themselves is to educate and a sustainable future can only be achieved through providing educational environments which themselves communicate ecologically sound messages.

In the case of Riverhead School, sustainability was incorporated into the design from the outset. The building has always been seen as part of its landscaped setting: built form and greenbelt forming an integrated approach. This conveys important messages to children in their formative years about mankind's relationship with the planet. The plan form of the building is simple—a large rectangle. This is both efficient and flexible, avoiding wasted circulation space and allowing the internal layouts to develop alongside future education methods. It could thereby prolong the useful life of the building, or even allow it to be used for other purposes. The deep plan reduces the external envelope of the building, cutting heat loss and reducing the quantity of materials needed. This is at no cost to those spaces requiring external elevations for access, light and air: all nine classrooms are in the optimum location, on the south side of the building. All benefit from full-height glazing, bringing in sunlight, providing views of the idyllic landscape, and allowing pupils to move between indoor and outdoor teaching areas. Additionally, the classrooms are screened from the noise and pollution of the busy A25, which lies to the north (see page 60).

Classrooms are generally too deep in plan to rely on just one facade for ventilation, yet to be efficient in use of circulation space the optimum arrangement is to have them arranged on either side of a central corridor. A solution to this is to form air ducts which draw air in at high level, on the corridor side of the classroom, and to discharge the stale air at roof level. At Trinity School a new classroom and laboratory wing uses passive vents to refresh air in the teaching spaces. Air is drawn in through louvres integrated into the external facades and windows can be opened as well. The building incorporates large areas of glazing to maximise natural light; on the south side this needs to be protected by external louvres to reduce thermal gain. The underside of the structural concrete slab is left exposed, so that it can act as a heat sink during the day, discharging this energy at night as the space cools. Acoustic panels provide visual contrast to the concrete and absorb sound. These principles were shown on the early concept sketch (left). The external expression of the building reflects these environmental concerns whilst relating to its context. Folded planes of stone and metal, and panels of glass, relate to the simple modernist expression in Portland stone and glass of the existing School buildings.

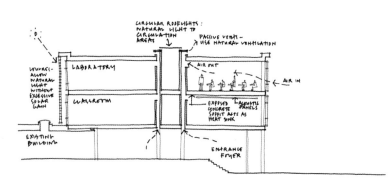

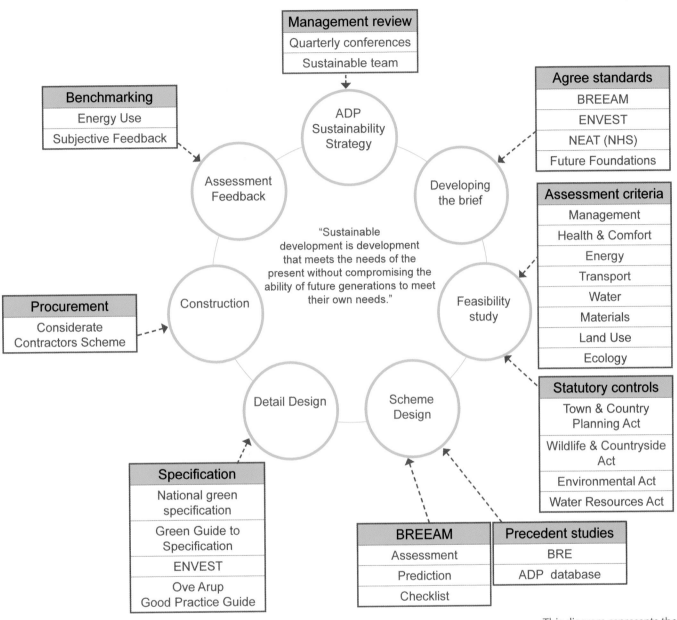

Management review
- Quarterly conferences
- Sustainable team

Benchmarking
- Energy Use
- Subjective Feedback

Agree standards
- BREEAM
- ENVEST
- NEAT (NHS)
- Future Foundations

Assessment criteria
- Management
- Health & Comfort
- Energy
- Transport
- Water
- Materials
- Land Use
- Ecology

Procurement
- Considerate Contractors Scheme

Statutory controls
- Town & Country Planning Act
- Wildlife & Countryside Act
- Environmental Act
- Water Resources Act

Specification
- National green specification
- Green Guide to Specification
- ENVEST
- Ove Arup Good Practice Guide

BREEAM
- Assessment
- Prediction
- Checklist

Precedent studies
- BRE
- ADP database

Circle diagram stages:
- ADP Sustainability Strategy
- Assessment Feedback
- Developing the brief
- Construction
- Feasibility study
- Detail Design
- Scheme Design

"Sustainable development is development that meets the needs of the present without compromising the ability of future generations to meet their own needs."

This diagram represents the sequence that a project passes through from inception to completion, including the evaluation process that we use to feed back into our own policies. At each stage there are more detailed issues to consider and our internal intranet version of this diagram has expanding sub-headings and links to the extensive further advice and guidance now available.

This is one of our procedures which has helped us achieve ISO 14001 accreditation, verifying our environmental management systems and our commitment to environmental aspects.

The northern side of the building is dominated by two winter gardens. These are top-lit by openable rooflights, which introduce sunlight and natural ventilation to the heart of the building. In this way, windows in the north-facing elevation can be kept minimal: small squares at desk height that provide a view out, but do not allow noise or cold air in. To avoid excessive solar gain, a series of horizontal steel rods span between the main ribs, thereby shading the large areas of glazing from direct sunlight. A grass roof was considered, but would have required a greater depth of soil, thus heavier steel work and larger foundations: all of which would consume more energy to construct and maintain. In contrast, Sedum is much 'leaner'; it has a greater tolerance of drought and supports a wider range of wildlife.

Although within the Green Belt, the school actually occupies a brownfield site, formerly used as a tip and as a contractor's compound when the A21 was built. The Building Research Establishment audited the project at design development stage, so that recommendations could be reviewed before the design was finalised. Care was taken in the selection of materials, and insulation values were maximised wherever possible. Underfloor heating, zoned to give user control, provides heat where it is most beneficial to the building's small users. The building benefits from natural light and ventilation, with classrooms opening out onto outdoor teaching areas. Openable rooflights to the classrooms provide natural light and ventilation. The building footprint is compact. The roof acts as a heat sink, and external louvres prevent excessive solar gain. Local and recycled materials have been used, such as crushed recycled glass instead of sand, for bedding the paving.

These architectural 'steps', aside from reducing costs, improving efficiency and potentially extending the life of the building, encourage the children who use the school every day to think about and live within this environment, sustainably. A green travel plan, with 'walking buses' where children are collected at specific 'stops', reaffirms this message and cuts carbon emissions from parents taking their children to school.

At the University of Derby, sustainability and low energy usage have been integrated into a new Faculty of Arts Design and Technology, right from the outset. The design is both functional and highly flexible, taking a very 'honest' approach to these issues. It uses local materials—such as Derbyshire red brick—and exposed concrete, as key features of the design. A sustainable approach has also been adopted, with whole life-cycle costing taken into consideration. Natural ventilation is employed throughout much of the building and storm waters are diverted to newly created reed beds for filtration—a direct response to the Grade I listed mill pond situated opposite.

Runoff from the roofs of the new faculty flows into the reed beds. Water can then percolate slowly into the surrounding ground, reducing the load on the sewerage system. The development will also create new habitats, enhancing the existing environment for the benefit of the University and the wider community. Reducing water consumption can be achieved through specification of fittings; low flush WCs and spray taps can be used in combination with grey water systems for garden irrigation and WC flushing. The treatment of grey water on site to allow it to be used as drinking water, although not currently an attractive option in terms of payback, may become more affordable as water costs rise and on larger scale projects.

Designing for buffering rainwater run-off can reduce flooding and provide an attractive external works design by selection of permeable materials and even balance ponds.

Student accommodation has long been a prime target for reducing energy costs as these buildings soak up a significant percentage of a university's energy bill, with each student able to increase energy consumption at will. At the University of Bath, ADP has created 355 units of undergraduate and postgraduate accommodation, located in a sensitive site on the edge of an existing campus adjacent to an Area of Outstanding Natural Beauty and to National Trust Land. The student residences have been designed with high quality and low life-cycle costs in mind. Concrete panel construction has been used for robustness, thermal mass and acoustic properties along with speed of construction. The sustainable approach was driven by the University's own policy, insisting on high standards and employing techniques such as solar shading and solar pre-heating of water.

A key element of the design development of the student residences was life-cycle costing. Using methodical analysis of options, elements were either incorporated into the design or rejected: this rigorous approach ensures that sustainable features are an integral part of the long-term plan for the building rather than just being gimmicks. In the case of this project at the University of Bath, solar pre-heating of water, insulation upgrades, and heat recovery from bathroom extracts were incorporated into the design, while photovoltaic cells and grey-water recycling were rejected on a life-cycle cost basis. This process was carried out with the expectation for the scheme to receive an "excellent" BREEAM rating, and by doing so the project would be one of only two student residence schemes in the country to achieve this result.

Barr Beacon is an important landmark in the Black Country and this visitor centre will form an important facility on the 'Green Bridge' Route. The building will provide information, exhibition and learning areas, refreshments and toilets. The impact of the building has been minimised by efficient space planning and by sinking the built form into the heathland, which will be banked up to the building and carried over its roof. One side will be fully glazed to take advantage of the panoramic views. A biomass boiler will provide heat with labyrinthine cooling/heating ensuring a balanced environment. External louvres will prevent excessive solar gain, and will fold shut against the building to secure it at night. Rainwater harvesting and use of grey water will assist further in the design of a highly sensitive, contextual and environmentally responsible building, with interactive displays providing accessible data on the building's performance in practice.

The West Campus project for the University of Birmingham provides flexible and efficient space which should maximise the life and usefulness of the building, which was rated 'Very Good' by BREEAM.

Materials can be selected with consideration to life-cycle costs. If appropriate, particular attention can be paid to those which score favourably with the BREEAM system (Green Guide to Materials Specification) which promotes the use of natural, recycled, reclaimed materials with a low embodied energy and those not associated with habitat destruction.

Where heavyweight construction methods are used, thermal mass can be exploited by introducing night-time ventilation for passive cooling. This can be combined with a heat recovering system to allow the re-use of heat within extract air. 'Super' insulation can be used without significantly increasing the external envelope thickness. Advances in the manufacture of insulation materials now allow denser, highly insulating materials to be produced. The thermal stability of the earth can be exploited to cool buildings in summer (when the earth is cooler than prevailing conditions) and to warm buildings in winter (when it is warmer). This technique is being used in a project at Canterbury

The Proudman Oceanographic Laboratory in Liverpool replaced the building envelope and services whilst retaining the main structural frame.

Christ Church University. Tubes carrying water are integrated into geothermal piles, carrying water deep into the earth, transferring heat and reducing the energy load on the building.

Heat reclamation can be utilised by recycling the heat from human bodies, electrical equipment and solar heat gains. This is only viable when the value of the heat recovered is more than the running costs of the heat exchanger or recovery equipment. Heat exchangers or recovery units transfer additional heat build up back into either water or air (depending on what is required) and this offsets against the generation of heat that would otherwise be required to compensate for the heat lost through extraction. Building services can be designed to match the flexible use patterns of academic departments including zoning and PIR controls. A sophisticated Building Management System can monitor energy and water use and space can be provided for segregation of waste for recycling.

Natural ventilation to vertical core areas can be provided using the passive stack principle. This in turn can be used to draw air through from areas off the vertical circulation providing a natural air flow. A system utilising proprietary precast concrete planks with integrated air paths provides closely controlled ventilation and openable windows can allow fine tuning of environmental conditions by the occupants. Heat recovery/exchange systems can be implemented to allow the reuse of heat within extract air and grey-water. This technique was employed at the University of Birmingham West Campus using the Swedish Termodeck system. The buildings are divided into four heating zones, consisting of one half of the basement and ground floor grouped together; the second half of the basement and ground floor; half the first and second floor grouped together and the second half of the first and second floor. The outcome was that an intensely used building with a high IT density does not need to be air conditioned. Termodeck floor slabs are both a structural component and a means of ducting ventilation through the building. Using this system enabled the building to secure a BREEAM rating of "Very Good".

Much building stock within the education environment is no longer efficiently fitted to suit its current purpose. Mid sixties and early seventies buildings are now at the end of their planned lifecycle. Skilled assessment of opportunities for adaptation, extension and remodelling of existing buildings can lead to innovative outcomes and where replacement is necessary recycling of land and materials should be fully considered.

The ultimate expression of this is in our work for the Natural Environment Research Council for the Proudman Oceanographic Laboratory (POL) where ADP challenged an assumption of full demolition of an exisiting building and instead proposed re-using the steel frame of an existing building on the site. The existing, redundant building, was carefully dismantled, with as much as possible of the original building, including the 1934 steel frame and foundations, retained. From the outset, we adopted a sustainable design approach, seeking to create a more natural environment that is in keeping with POL's work. The new building has been designed to incorporate features such as natural ventilation, night purge cooling and sensor-operated lighting and as a result, achieved a high environmental rating from the Building Research Establishment (BRE).

At the Proudman Oceanographic Laboratory, generous floor to ceiling heights allowed for high level opening windows permitting natural light and ventilation to penetrate deep into the open plan office areas, minimising the need for artificial lighting. A small rainwater recycling system reduced the water consumption for toilets and solar collectors provide domestic hot water.

The practice has seen huge changes, particularly in the building industry and how the profession operates, over the past forty years. We have shown how ADP began and evolved, and examined a large body of our current work, for the education sector. This brings its own unique challenges, both in how to organise a service to meet its particular requirements and in meeting the technical needs of a wide range of specialist building types.

ADP has always shown a concern to integrate its buildings into their settings. Successful application of this skill has brought increasingly challenging commissions in sensitive surroundings. We have avoided momentary stylistic fashions, preferring to maintain a logical process of understanding and analysis, matching a design solution to the needs of the client and the special characteristics of a specific location.

This approach sits very happily alongside an environmentally responsible approach, and in this final chapter we have outlined our approach to sustainable design. As we look ahead there is no doubt that the context in which we work will continue to change, and the need to design responsibly, sensitively and logically will continue to match ADP's philosophy.

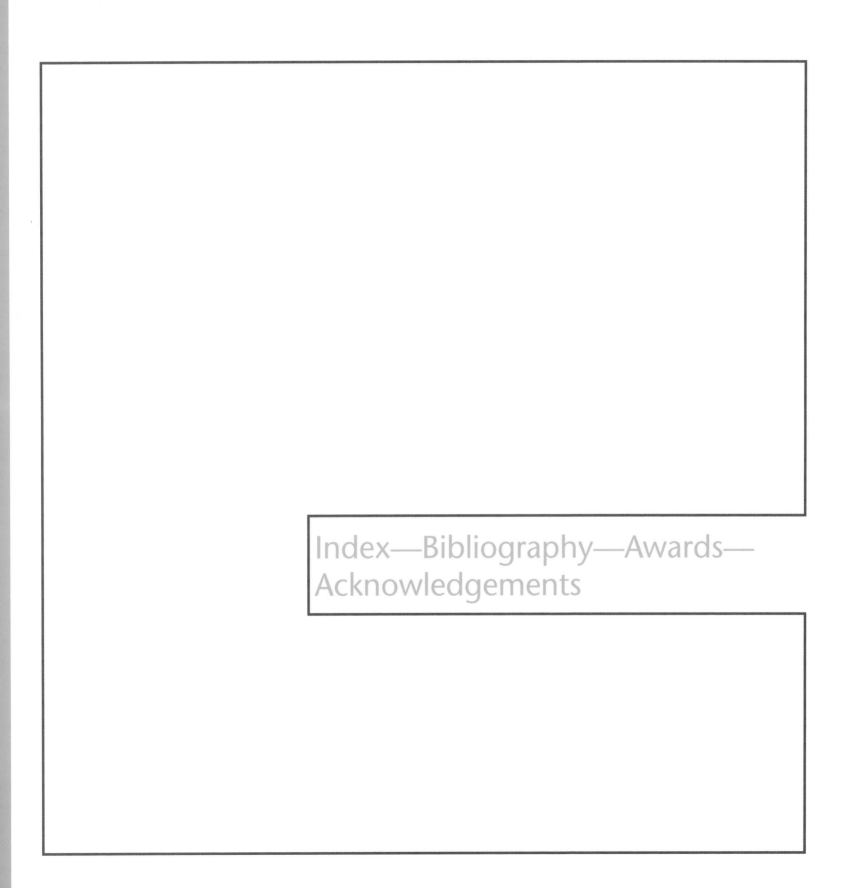

Index

Bibliography

2007

May
Sunday Times Homes
Redevelopment of Royal Masonic School
Comer Homes

Building Design
Study in Refurbishment
Oxford Castle

April
Building Magazine
Canterbury learning centre
Canterbury Christ Church University

March
You and Your Wedding
Perfect Venue Guide—Urban Hip
Oxford Castle

Slough Observer
Muslim School Design Unveiled
Slough Islamic School

Sustain
New Student Residences Scheme
University of Bath

Mix Interiors
Aston Promise
Aston Business School Conference Centre

January
AJ Plus
Canterbury Christ Church University
Building Design
Canterbury's Green Wings
Canterbury Christ Church University

2006

DfES—Every Child Matters:
Primary Capital Programme
"Building primary schools at the heart of
the community"
Riverhead Infants School

December
Kent Messenger
University's £30m flagship Building
Canterbury Christ Church University

November
Building Magazine
Through the Keyhole
"My Council"
Slough Council

July
AT Handbook
Architects Design Partnership
Wolfson Centre for Medical Education
The University of Birmingham

April
Natural Stone Specialist
Jailhouse Rock
Oxford Castle

AT Handbook
Ealing Institute of Media
Ealing Institute of Media
Ealing, Hammersmith and West
London College

March
Shared Interest (English Heritage)
Oxford Castle
Oxford Castle

Building
'Parliament to get new Entrance'
New Visitor Access Improvements,
Palace of Westminster

February
School Building
'New facility offers exciting opportunities in
film and TV'
Ealing Institute of Media
Ealing, Hammersmith and West London
College

Building Magazine
'High Performance Arts'
Faculty of Arts, Design and Technology,
University of Derby

2005

December
Building Magazine
Ealing Classic
Ealing Institute of Media,
Ealing, Hammersmith and West London
College

November
Public Sector Construction
'Derby Days'
Faculty of Arts, Design and Technology,
University of Derby

October
Building for Education
'Outer Space for Sixth Form College'
King Edward VI College, Stourbridge

September
The Architects' Journal
Sketchbook
Illustrations of the University of Sussex
by Roger FitzGerald

June/July
School Building
Collingwood College
Review of new Sixth Form Centre

May
Architecture Today
'Missing Link'
New Sixth Form Centre,
Collingwood College

Building Magazine
Civic Trust Awards Supplement
Review of Roffey Park Institute
(Commendation, 2005 Civic Trust Awards)

The Architects' Journal
AJ100
ADP ranks 33 in this years' rankings

January
Building Design
"Tone up for 50/50 Charter"
Update: week 3 Spotlight on ADP

Building Design
"Sail of the century"
James Middleton-Stewart's fundraising

2004

December
Lifetimes
"From Prison to Penthouse"
ADP constructs luxury apartments
at the heart of the Oxford Castle
Heritage Project

November
Mix Interiors
"Check In"
ADP's impressive refit of Apex Plaza, Reading

Hampshire Chronicle
"Market Hall restored to former glory"
Succesful renovation of Old Market House

October
Sleeper—'The Drawing Board'
'Malmaison Oxford'
Review of ADP's redevelopment of Oxford
Castle site to create a Malmaison Hotel

Oxford Times—In Business
"Revival of castle site underway"
Review of Oxford Castle Heritage Project

September
Hospital Development
Feature: "Focused group"
Delivering patient-centred healthcare for
Macmillan Cancer Relief

Ealing Gazette
"Institute has media in frame"
Review of Ealing, Hammersmith and West
London College's new
Centre of Vocational Excellence

August
Hospital Bulletin
"Parallel training for students"
Student nurses training at the University
of Wolverhampton School of Health enjoy
two new modern fully equipped buildings,
specially designed by ADP

June
The Birmingham Post
"ADP settles into new home"
Launch of new offices in historic jewellery
quarter

The Birmingham Post
"Double boost for nurses' training"
Nurses' training at the Wolverhampton
School of Health has been enhanced by the
completion of two state-of-the-art buildings

The Birmingham Post
"Four into one proves successful combination"
ADP's refurbishment of University House

The Birmingham Post
"Landmark relocation for Proudman"
New 43,000 sq m research facility in the
University of Liverpool's city centre precinct

May
Building for Education
Cover Story: £33m refurbishment of
historic school
ADP's 8-year programme of phased
refurbishment

March
Health Estate Journal
"Convincing case for patient-centred
buildings: Creating a healing environment
with appropriate building design"

The Architects' Journal
"AJ 100 2004"
Architects Design Partnership LLP ranked 31
in the AJ top 100 architects

2003

March
Architektur + Wettbewerbe
(Architecture and Competitions)
'Ganztagsschulen' (All-day Schools)
Riverhead Infants School

Design Council and DfES
Furniture for the Future—New ideas
for tomorrow's classroom, Riverhead
Infants School

July
The Architects' Journal
"Open For Business"
Roffey Park Management Institute

2002

October
The Architects' Journal
"Under One Roof"
Riverhead Infants School

September
Building Specifier
"Learning Curves"
Riverhead Infants School

2001

Building Research Establishment—
Best Practice Programme
Design Advice: Towards Greener Buildings
"Learning to be green"
Riverhead Infants School

January
The Architects' Journal
"ADP is top of the class with 'green' school"
Riverhead Infants School

1997

September
The Architects' Journal
"Winning Stable: Five Star Stabling"
Polo Stables, Oxfordshire

1994

Architecture in Conservation
"The Way Forward - Approach"
New Swimming Pool Extension to Private
House, Oxford

August
The Architects' Journal
"College extension balances pragmatism
and respect"
King Street Development, Christ's College

July
Museums Journal
"Brewing, Biscuits, Baking and Bayeux"
Reading Town Hall

1993

June
The Architects' Journal
"Flexible, low-key hospice for residents
and daycare"
Lions Hospice, Dartford

1989

November
Building Design
"Principles in Perspective"
New Swimming Pool Extension to
Private House, Oxford

April
Building
Building Dossier: "Private Swimming Pool"
New Swimming Pool Extension to
Private House, Oxford

1988

Concrete Quarterly
"Riverside Delight"
New Swimming Pool Extension to
Private House, Oxford

1982

June
Building
Building Dossier: "Fine Definition"
Institute of Virology

February
The Architects' Journal
Water Colours
Engineering Research Centre for the Water
Research Centre, Swindon

1977

August
Building
Building Dossier: "The Roberts Building
for OUP"
The Roberts Building, Oxford University Press

1976

January
Building
Building Dossier: "Flats, St Catherine's,
Oxford"
Graduate Flats for St Catherine's
College, Oxford

Awards

2007

RIBA Award
Oxford Castle
RICS South East Overall Award
Oxford Castle
**RICS South East Regeneration Projects—
Overall Winner**
Oxford Castle
MIPIM Hotel and Tourism Award
Malmaison Hotel, Oxford Castle
**Civic Trust 'Outstanding Centre
Vision Award'**
Oxford Castle

2006

**The Guildford Society Design Awards,
New Build Category**
Postgraduate Medical School University
of Surrey
Oxford Preservation Trust Commendation
Lincoln College EPA Science Centre

2005

**Haringey Design Awards
(Education Commendation)**
Highgate School
**Guildford Borough Heritage and
Environment Awards**
Postgraduate Medical School
University of Surrey
Civic Trust Award (Commendation)
Roffey Park Management Institute

2004

**National BUR Awards for the
Flat Roofing Alliance: New Build:
Best Project**
Riverhead Infants School, Kent

2003

NHS Award for Environmental Design
Roxburghe House, Dundee
NHS Partnership Award
Northampton General Hospital
Best Public Building, Kent Design Awards
Riverhead Infants School, Kent
Civic Trust Award (Commendation)
Riverhead Infants School, Kent

1997

David Unwin Award
Christ's College, Cambridge
Guildford Heritage Trust
Academic Building, University of Surrey

1993

Oxford Preservation Trust Award
Oxford University Press

1992

Civic Trust Award
Turkey Court, Maidstone

1990

RIBA Regional Award
Reading Town Hall

1990

Civic Trust Award
Reading Town Hall
RIBA Regional Award
Private swimming pool, Oxfordshire

1988

Concrete Society Award
Private swimming pool, Oxfordshire
Oxford Preservation Trust Award
Mansfield College

Oxford Preservation Trust Award
Zacharias, Cornmarket Street
RIBA Regional Award
Christ Church Oxford
RIBA National Award
Christ Church Oxford

1987

Vale of White Horse Design Award
Pulpit House, Abingdon

1984

Oxford Preservation Trust Award
Morris Garage, Longwall Street

1983

Brick Development Association Award
Institute of Virology Oxford

1982

Oxford Preservation Trust Award
Frewin Hall, Oxford

1981

Oxford Preservation Trust Award
18/24 New Inn Hall Street

ROYAL ACADEMY SUMMER EXHIBITION

2003

Roffey Park Institute, Horsham

2002

Riverhead Infants School, Sevenoaks

1989

Private Swimming Pool extension to private
house, Oxford

Acknowledgements

ADP would like to acknowledge the considerable contributions made to the text for the education section by Professor Roy Newton, former Pro Vice-Chancellor, University of Wolverhampton and Angela Nash of the University of Wolverhampton.

Photographic credits are as follows:

12
The Beatles (Courtesy of PA Photos)

13
Denmark House (Mike Thomas)
Jesus College Oxford (Henk Snoek; Henk Snoek/RIBA Library Photograph Collection)

14
Old Members' Building, Jesus College (BJ Harris)

15
The Mitchell Building, University College Graduate Common Rooms, Workshop and Kitchen Staff facilities (Henk Snoek; Henk Snoek/RIBA Library Photograph Collection)

16–17
Institute of Hydrology (Henk Snoek; Henk Snoek/RIBA Library Photograph Collection)

18
Hydraulics Research, Wallingford

19
Engineering Centre, Swindon (Richard Bryant)

20–21
Engineering Centre, Swindon (Richard Bryant)
Christ Church Oxford (Simon Chapman)

24–25
St Margaret's Somerset Hospice (Nigel Rigden)

27
Oriental Pearl Restaurant (Jonathan Moore)
Brunel Central Lecture Building (Martin Cleveland)

28
Aston Business School Conference Centre (Jonathan Moore)

29
Aston Business School Conference Centre (Jonathan Moore)

32
Western House Primary School (Jonathan Moore)

35
Net Shape Building, University of Birmingham (VIEW; Peter Cook/VIEW)

36–37
Ealing, Hammersmith and West London College (Jonathan Moore)

40
Highgate School (Jonathan Moore)

41
Highgate School (Jonathan Moore)

43
Cokethorpe School (Jerry Moeran, Studio Edmark; Studio Edmark Photography)

44–46
University of Birmingham, West Campus (Jonathan Moore)

58
Canterbury Road Council School (Courtesy of Essex Records Office)

59
Image courtesy of Collingwood College

61
Riverhead School—boy peeking through window (VIEW; Hufton+Crow/VIEW)
Riverhead School—classroom and playground (Ray Hardinge)

64
St Olave's Grammar School (Courtesy of St Olave's Grammar School)

65
St Olave's Grammar School (Jonathan Moore)

66
University of Birmingham, Computer Clusters (VIEW; Peter Cook/VIEW)

66–69
University of Birmingham, School of Sport and Exercise Science (Jonathan Moore)

70
Aston Business School Conference Centre (Jonathan Moore)

71
Physics Media Services, University of Oxford

73
University of Birmingham Medical School (Jonathan Moore)

74–75
Austin Pearce Building, University of Surrey (VIEW; Peter Cook/VIEW)

76–77
University of Birmingham Medical School
(Jonathan Moore)

78–79
Aston Business School Conference Centre
(Jonathan Moore)

82
Christ's Hospital (Paul Mellor; Paul Mellor
Photography)

83
Christ's Hospital (Morley von Sternberg)

84
Christ's Hospital (Paul Mellor; Paul Mellor
Photography)

85
St Edwards School (VIEW; William Fife/
VIEW)

86–87
University of Oxford Swimming Pool (Courtesy
of Kingerlee Ltd)

90
Centre of Vocational Excellence, Ealing
(Jon Nicol Photography)

93
Brunel Central Lecture Building
(Martin Cleveland)

98
University of Birmingham West Campus
(Jonathan Moore)

100
King's College, University of Cambridge
(Mike Morley)

101
Pompidou Centre
(Courtesy of Photos Schmidt)

102–103
Private Swimming Pool (Tony Weller)

111
Oxford Castle (Morley von Sternberg)

113
Oxford Castle (Morley von Sternberg)

114
Oxford Castle (Morley von Sternberg)

116
Oxford Castle (Morley von Sternberg)

119
Aston Business School Conference Centre
(Jonathan Moore)

121
Christ's Hospital (Morley von Sternberg)

125–127
Christs College Cambridge (Iain Graham)

128–129
Reading Town Hall (VIEW; VIEW Pictures/
Peter Cook)

131
Highgate School (Jonathan Moore)

132–133
Nissan Institute (Charlotte Wood)

134
Yorkshire Dales (Frantisek Staud)

135
Chatsworth House (Chris Simpson)

136–7
Roffey Park Institute (VIEW; Edmund Sumner/
VIEW Pictures)
Roffey Park—cladding and render detail
(Nick Woodcock, Architects Design Partnership
LLP/Nick Woodcock)

138
Roffey Park Institute (VIEW; Edmund Sumner/
VIEW Pictures)
Roffey Park Institute—interiors (Barry Boxall)

144
Riverhead Infants School—sedum roof (Image
courtesy of Bauder Ltd)
Riverhead Infants School—school field (Ray
Hardinge)

146–147
Polo Stables (Tim Soar; Timothy Soar
Photography)

149–150
Oxford Science Park (Paul Harmer
Photography)

151
Oxford Science Park (details) (Mike Thomas)

153
Sir John Soane Museum (Eugene Reid,
Architects Design Partnership LLP)

156
Old Market House, Winchester (Images
courtesy of Strutt and Parker)

157
Brunel Central Lecture Building
(Martin Cleveland)

162
Trinity School, Croydon (Jonathan Moore)

167
University of Birmingham, West Campus
(Jonathan Moore)

168
Proudman Oceanographic Laboratory,
University of Liverpool (Jonathan Moore)

170
Proudman Oceanographic Laboratory,
University of Liverpool (Jonathan Moore)

173
Birch trees (Courtesy of Boston Globe/Landov
Media; John Tlumacki)

180
Brunel Central Lecture Building
(Martin Cleveland)

Black Dog Publishing Limited
Unit 4.4 Tea Building
56 Shoreditch High Street
London
E1 6JJ

Tel: +44 (0)20 7613 1922
Fax: +44 (0)20 7613 1944
Email: info@blackdogonline.com

www.blackdogonline.com

British Library Cataloguing-in-Publication Data.

A CIP record for this book is available from the British Library.

ISBN 10: 1-904772-71-4
ISBN 13: 978-1-904772-71-2

Black Dog Publishing is an environmentally responsible company.

Education and Contextualism is printed on Garda Matt 170 gsm, an
acid-free paper made with cellulose from certified forests, plantations
and well managed forests.

architecture art design
fashion history photography
theory and things

www.blackdogonline.com